Heart and Mind
What the Bible Says About Learning

Heart and Mind

What the Bible Says About Learning

Ruth Beechick

Fenton, Michigan 48430

ISBN 0-88062-173-7
Printed in the United States of America

Contents

Introduction, First Edition

This book, as all books, has a story behind it. Here is the story of how it came to be.

Learning has been my lifelong hobby, as well as my work. I do it, read it, teach it, study it, and write it. But most of the time there has been a dissonance in my view of theory. As with all Christians, I sat in university education classes and tried to understand, but something was always missing. In the "rat" classes, there was no human will or purpose. In the "couch" classes, there was no God or other reality outside the person and his relationships. The books and theories never seemed to describe what I was doing in my own learning and teaching.

In my work I felt something intensely human that was not described in the psychology books. When I taught reading to people with learning problems, I, of course, knew the reading process well and understood something about each person's problem, and had at hand numerous methods to use. But none of these was the main ingredient in the remarkable learning that often happened with these students. They wanted to learn. Sometimes it took a while to work through the barriers left from past failures, but underneath could always be found a strong desire to know how to read. And I wanted them to learn. That is what we built on—their hearts and my heart. Teacher and student in intense human encounter.

Later, when I had more time to think about this, I realized that we need a theory of learning based on the Bible. The shortcomings of secular theories are due mostly to their various secular views of man. We Christians have a higher view of man. We attribute to him God-like qualities—an immaterial soul, heart, mind or personality. Some of us may not be able to describe these very clearly in the way that science, logic, or theology would have it, but we believe in them anyway.

So I determined to see what the Bible said about learning. From my theologian son I learned the difference between English concordances and Greek and Hebrew concordances. I borrowed his hefty books and began filling papers with my studies of heart, mind, teaching, learning and related words. This search was proceeding during the limited time I could give it. Then one day I struck gold. No prospector could be more excited at a vein of high-grade ore. In the psychology section of a library's stacks I was pursuing a favorite hobby—browsing and picking up books I thought I would read. My eye fell on a title, *A System of Biblical Psychology*. I pulled the book off the shelf, noted that it had been checked out only twice in the fifteen years the library had owned it, and added it to my pile of books.

At home I began to assay my find and that's when I first realized what treasure I had. Franz Delitzsch, I learned, more than a century ago had pondered some of the same topics I ponder today. I soon realized I needed more than a library copy of this treasure, so I ordered my own. Delitzsch had already done much of the work I wanted to do, particularly in digging out the Bible teaching on *heart*. And his great theological mind did it better than I could, anyway. So you will find much of Delitzsch reflected in this book.

Now, I don't think secular learning theories are entirely wrong. I have profited from studying them, too. I am particularly indebted to two educational psychologists who themselves were dissatisfied with simply stimulus-response theory, needs theory, or any other one-factor explanation of how people learn. John A.R. Wilson and Mildred C.

Robeck developed a model with three levels and two sides, which reflects more of the complexity in human learning. I liked their model for the most part, but I couldn't help feeling that even here something was not quite right. From my Christian perspective the base seemed missing altogether, and there were other problems.

If we start from the Bible, I believe we can supply the missing base, and work out other problems, too, in learning theory. That's the story of this book.

As a help to readers who wish to pursue particular topics further, I have included an annotated bibliography. This is suggestive, only. With the numerous books available and with more constantly appearing, a comprehensive current listing would not be possible here.

My hope for this book is that it will stimulate thinking among Christians interested in education and that it will keep us moving along a biblical course.

Ruth Beechick
1982

Note: The first edition was titled
A Biblical Psychology of Learning.

Introduction, Second Edition

The most exciting development in learning theory since the first edition of this book is the continuing research on the heart. As to the physical heart, the Lacey husband and wife team mentioned in the first edition have extended their research on how the heart "talks" to the brain rather than only the brain talking to the heart and other physical organs. And Paul Pearsall, an organ transplant surgeon, has begun and continues publishing his research and anecdotes about organ transplant recipients.

As to *heart* in the Bible, this research, too, has been greatly extended until now this book contains the most complete research on this topic to be found anywhere. Kenneth Clark and Jack A. Noble, at Tennessee Temple Seminary, expanded the research which was only begun and outlined in Chapter 3 of the first edition of this book. They found that *heart* is used most often with a cognitive meaning, that is thinking, speaking, meditating and so forth. The meaning of physical heart is used less than any other Bible meanings. Details and data from their research are given in Appendix A.

The years intervening between these two editions also saw the burgeoning of the homeschool movement. Parents, even when afraid and intimidated by our society, have achieved remarkable results in their teaching. For the most part they have lacked formal teacher training, yet their results far outstrip the results of our government schooling institutions. This has to be due to the heart-to-heart approach that parents naturally use with their children. They use any curriculum or no curriculum; they use popular methods or homemade methods; yet they overwhelmingly produce superior results. Early in the movement, a researcher announced that he was going to measure the results of using various curriculums and various methods, and then tell homeschoolers the best ones to use. But he had set an impossible task.

American education research began about 1900 using the statistical methods then used in agriculture research. That is, you treat one field this way and one field that way and see which gets the best results. Education proved not as easy to measure as agriculture, so much of the early research was on memorizing, which was comparatively easy to measure. What they learned about memory is useful, and is included in this book, but educators soon realized that memory methods had limited use and they worked on developing other theories.

B.F. Skinner was probably the greatest education name of the twentieth century, from the 1930s to the 1950s. His belief was that of an evolutionist—that man is not someone inside the body, but that the body *is* the man. Following Skinner, other theorists arose who tried to improve on his work. Mostly, they wanted something more complex than the stimulus-response mechanism developed by Skinner. Through about the 1960s was the heyday of education theorists.

In more recent years, not so much is happening. In fact, we seem more locked into the evolution philosophy that man can be studied just as machines can be studied. Some theories, though they may not mention Skinner or behaviorism, nevertheless are based on that view of man. Thus, studying behaviorism helps to give a clearer understanding of other theories which may not use that word, but are non-biblical nevertheless.

How does our mind work? How do we learn? Is our

heart an important part of this process? We explore these questions in this book. Major theories are outlined and described, and then the refreshing, freeing, heart theory from the Bible is contrasted with them all.

Ruth Beechick
2004

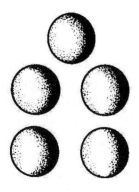

1

The Body-Soul Question

"What is heart?" wrote a philosophy professor in the margin of my paper. He was not looking for an answer; he was marking what he thought was a mistake. Heart was not real. I could not write about it for his class. In physiology, maybe. But not in educational psychology. I had to do my reasoning and reach my conclusions by some other route.

But it is a good question. What is heart?

In our folklore and our common sense we have a ready answer. Some things we just know in our hearts. We might think with our heads, but it is our hearts that tell us we are persons. By our hearts we know there is a God. In our hearts we love and hate.

When we are trying to be psychological and scientific we do not have such ready answers. The major theories taught in secular psychology classes leave no room for heart.

Behaviorist theories see man as a machine—a computer-like machine—which responds according to what is programmed into it. There is no person inside the machine with heart or will or any such thing to affect what it does.

9

Only the programming determines how it responds. Behaviorism is at the base of all modern theories by evolutionists, though they do not use this word much anymore, because of this belief that humans are only material. Nothing spiritual is inside.

Humanists sound a little better in their writings. They believe there is something uniquely human about man, and they have their varying theories about what it is. Man has evolved something or other beyond what animals have. It might be language ability. It might be "time-binding"— the ability to think about past history and future planning. It might be culture—ability to create and enjoy art, literature, and so forth. But whatever it is, it has biological roots. All we have to do is explain biology in terms of chemistry, then explain chemistry in terms of molecular behavior, and so on down. When we have man reduced to his scientific lowest terms we will have figured out what is uniquely human about him.

Christians look up, not down. God created man in His own image and breathed the breath of life into him. So to learn what is unique about man we need to find out what that image of God means. When we look to the Bible one inescapable fact about man is his heart. The word is used almost 1000 times. This is *lêb* or *lêbab* in Hebrew, and *kardia* in Greek.

One thousand times! Some people say, "Well, that's just because the ancients thought the heart was the seat of affections and so they wrote that way." We are supposed to be smarter now. We should use our modern idiom and say *mind* instead of *heart*. And by mind we really mean brain. Everybody knows we understand with our brain. And we love and hate with our brain.

But God said heart.

We could respond to the argument by asking whether the ancients might have been at least as smart as we.

Common wisdom may have been passed down to us through language, so that we still say, "Get to the heart of the matter." Why don't we say, "Let's get to the brain of the matter?" Why do we put our hearts into our work? Why do we lose heart, or learn by heart, or have heart-to-heart talks? Is this all nonsense, or do we instinctively cling to some deeply rooted truth?

Well, says another argument, heart is figurative. As the physiological heart is central to the body, so the figurative heart is central to emotions.

To this argument we have to exclaim that this is certainly unusual in literature. It is entirely out of balance to always speak of something figuratively and never use its true name. The word *brain* is not found in the Bible even once. Now if we moderns are right in saying that brain really carries on most of the functions the ancients attributed to heart, it seems that God would have slipped the word in at least one or two times and clued us in on the true nature of man.

What about *mind*? Could *heart* in the Bible mean *mind* instead of brain? Well, mind does appear in the Bible, but only a fraction as often as heart. It occurs less than 100 times in the English Bible. And those occurrences are spread over about a dozen different words in the original languages. That dilutes the ratio, so that for any one word translated as *mind*, the Greek and Hebrew words translated as *heart* occur about 100 times more often. This in itself should tell us something about the importance of heart.

The philosophy professor who would not allow the word *heart* in his class also would be particular about how one used the word *mind*. He was the kind who denied anything immaterial in man. For him, man had no soul, mind, heart, spirit, or anything beyond the body. The history of brain research shows at times a prevailing view that there may be an immaterial aspect to man, something beyond what the scalpel and microscope reveal. But the view does not stay on top. Scientists quickly scramble around for ways to explain the unexplained and put mind back into the brain and make it material again.

For a long time—in the 1800s and into the 1900s—a narrow localization theory of brain was predominant. This was developed by studying damaged brains. If a certain brain area was damaged and the person could not remember where he was or where he came from, that area was labeled "memory of place." If another person with a damaged area could not read, his area was labeled "reading." By this means, researchers made maps of the brain and labeled the pieces. They were helped later by brain surgeons. During brain surgery the patient is often kept conscious, as brain tissues do not experience pain, and researchers can stimulate various exposed parts of the brain and observe what part of the body moves, or ask the patient what sensation it gives him. Through such work the brain maps became very intricate. They were put into textbooks and until rather recently this localization theory was the "scientific truth" about brain.

The non-soul people had it made. Didn't all the textbooks explain how the brain works? They did not need concepts such as mind or heart to explain man. There it all was, on the brain maps.

But cracks appeared in the theory. Someone whose reading area was damaged learned to read anyway. People were doing lots of things that the maps could not explain. It was time for the soul people to say, "See? I told you so. There must be an immaterial mind and not only a material brain."

The non-soul people did not give up easily. They began embracing a more complex theory. It can be called the level theory. The brain is like a computer and operates on many levels. The lowest, "hardware," level is where the neurons fire off their electrochemical charges across the gaps between one another. When somebody learns a bit of something, a particular chain of neurons gets organized with the learning. That little unit, and the zillions of similar units in the brain are a step higher than the hardware level. The units get bunched into systems, and those into systems of systems, and so on to an uncountable number of higher levels, as well as an incredible complexity of crisscrossing among systems.

We had an explanation for anything that humans could do. The non-soul people were on top again. It was pretty mechanical after all.

Are there cracks in this theory? Some people think so. A recent proposal is that brain is tuned in to the universe, having access to a realm far beyond time and space. Remarkable. Now if they would just say there is a spirit within a man which can commune with the God who made him, they'd be on the soul side. But it is not in the nature of science to side with the soul people. At least in our time.

While some mavericks suggest a mystical sounding view, most scientists continue on the reductionist route. Neurons are now seen to contain ribonucleic acid (RNA). The RNA molecule contains DNA and possibly more subunits which would have, mathematically speaking, an astronomical number of arrangements. A hypothesis now is that each bit of information makes a change in an RNA molecule in the brain.

Isaac Asimov said that the behaviorists must be right in their principle that all human behavior can be brought down to a mechanical pattern of nerve cells and hormones because, "Unless we postulate the existence of something beyond the physical-chemical (something like abstract "mind" or "soul") we are reduced to finding the answer to even the highest human abilities somewhere among the cells of the nervous system or among the chemicals in the blood—exactly where we find the lowest" (*The Human Brain*. New York: New American Library, 1965, page 328). It is significant that Asimov used the word *reduced*. It sounds as though it is in some way unpalatable to him, but since he would not postulate soul, he was reduced to looking at chemicals. William Glasser, in the closing statement of his brilliant book, *Stations of the Mind* (New York: Harper and Row, 1981), wrote that if we continue to probe the brain it may "shed some light on the ancient philosophical question—which we have avoided in this book because so far it has no answer—who is it who builds my inner world?"

Belief that mind can cause body disorders has been increasing. More and more doctors—and patients, too—accept the idea of psychosomatic illness. This term, which should mean "soul-body," is often used actually to mean "body-body." That is, people may write about how the psyche or mind, when out of whack, causes diseases of the body. But a careful reading of what they mean by mind reveals that it is body, too. It has to be explained by neurons and molecules. Or if not, it must be reduced further yet, and someday when all the answers are in we will no longer need our superstitious belief in soul.

Glasser spent several years reading brain books, trying to find a theory that related brain to daily experience. He could not accept the usual stimulus-response idea that our behavior is determined from without. He finally found what he wanted in *Behavior: The Control of Perception*, by William T. Powers (Aldine, 1973). He consulted with Powers to build Powers' theory into his own Reality Therapy system and to write it for laymen. The result of this collaboration is Glasser's *Stations* book. These two men almost believe in personality. The person can control what he does. He does not *have* depression or *get* headaches. Instead, he depresses or headaches. The words are verbs, because the person is doing it.

In this control system, the brain controls for input, not output. This is difficult to understand at first. It is contrary to the more common belief that we behave in ways to cope with what happens to us from the outside: if our parents did not love us we fight back at the world in various ways. In control psychology we have perceptions in our brain of what we want, and we control input to match the perceptions whenever possible. When this is not possible, there is "error." Error drives us to various behaviors to reduce the error. Too much error and the person may choose to headache or cold or even schizophrene.

Now a key question would seem to be, "How does a particular perception get into a person's head?" Glasser's answer is, "No one exactly knows" (page 43). Past experiences add up. But if that is all we have, we are right back at the behaviorist view that what happens to us determines how we behave.

Some other researchers interested in the psychosomatic question are Drs. John I. and Beatrice C. Lacey. This husband and wife team researched the role of heart, and they found heart and brain to interact in surprising ways. One of their findings concerns what we might call "stiff necks." The Bible tells us about stiff necks too. The Lord was angry with the Israelites because they were stiffnecked (Exodus 32:9; Deuteronomy 9:6,13). Moses told them to circumcise their hearts (!) and not be stiffnecked. Their descendants in the time of the kings also "hardened" their necks (II Kings 17:14).

Now in the neck is the carotid sinus. This is one of two major origination points of nerve fibers which sense heart messages from the walls of the main arteries. In other words, this sinus area is a transmitting station where heart messages are converted into nerve messages which can be understood by the brain.

The other major transmitting station is near the heart

itself. A main artery travels through the neck carrying its messages from the heart. At the transmitting station the vagus nerve picks up the messages by sensing pressure and other complex signals from the artery wall. The home office of the vagus nerve is not far off, as it is in the hindbrain, the lower part of the brain. The vagus nerve takes home a message and the hindbrain uses it in its complex task of regulating the body operations.

Powers and Glasser have the forebrain telling the hindbrain whether to headache or to operate normally. But the Laceys have messages coming in from the heart too. And there may be a saboteur in the transmitting station. His technique is to stiffen the sinus wall. This causes the artery wall to be less elastic and the nerve has trouble picking up a message. The Bible indicates that the person himself can be the saboteur. In an act of mind over body, he can stiffen or harden his neck. (We will look at more of the Laceys' heart research in Chapter 3.) This stiff neck research is reported in "Somatopsychic Effects of Interoception" in *Research in the Psychobiology of Human Behavior* (ed. Eugene Meyer III and Joseph V. Brady. Baltimore: Johns Hopkins University Press, 1979).

The body-soul or body-mind question is an ancient one. For a long time, philosophers and psychologists have argued over it. Relative newcomers to the argument are computer people. Believe it or not, books have argued that computers will eventually have something akin to "mind," and they are so serious about it that other books are written to refute them.

In this book I do not intend to be theological about soul—or about mind, heart, personhood, or spirit. I leave to the theologians their analyses of the spiritual side of man. Just one point concerns us here: man does have his immaterial side. That is important for learning theory. That is where current popular learning theories go wrong.

Behaviorism, for instance, was developed largely from the study of rats, pigeons, and other laboratory animals. And why not? If man is just as personless as a pigeon, it ought to be good enough to study how pigeons learn and then transfer the principles to teaching people. The major principles in behaviorism concern environment—the stimuli and rewards. Learning is measured by outer responses only. There is no person inside to be concerned with.

If we believe that man has his immaterial part, it makes a great deal of difference in our learning theory. A person's determination, will, understanding, and a lot of other things we might call "heart" enter into the matter. We would not expect to locate these in the body, since they are immaterial. But we must include them, nevertheless, in a learning theory built on a view of man made in the image of God.

Though the body is not the person, the body houses the person. And in ways we may never understand, the person must use the body. Therefore, we do not discount modern research. Everything we learn about the brain, for instance, helps us understand better how people learn. We just need to remember that brain is not all. Something immaterial that we call "mind" is involved too. Shall we say that mind is behind brain? Above it? Shall we say that mind uses brain? However we conceive it, as Christians we recognize mind. And we know that it is not simply another word for brain. We side with the soul philosophers on this.

When it comes to heart we need similar thinking. Does the immaterial heart work through the material one? Non-Christian researchers in the various branches of psychology are not likely to figure that out for us. They will be too bent on finding naturalistic explanations. Robert Jastrow, an astronomer, explained the reason clearly in an article for *New York Times Magazine* ("Have Astronomers Found God?" June 25, 1978), reprinted in Reader's Digest and

17

elsewhere. Jastrow wrote while the big-bang theory was still well accepted among scientists, and he pointed out that it seemed to imply a Creator behind the bang. An M.I.T. professor said, "I would like to reject the big-bang theory, but I have to face the facts." Jastrow commented, "This reaction and similar responses by other astronomers have an odd ring of feeling and emotion. They come from the heart, whereas you would expect such judgments to come from the brain. Why? I think part of the answer is that scientists cannot bear the thought of a natural phenomenon that cannot be explained. There is a kind of religion in science. . . ."

Notice that this astronomer had no trouble using the word *heart* in contrast to brain. If he were a psychologist he might have.

The beautiful ending of Jastrow's article is worth quoting here. It applies to our topic of heart and soul just as well as his topic of astronomy. Jastrow wrote that when a scientist lives his life by faith in the power of reason and comes to an insurmountable barrier to further research, it is like a bad dream. He finds, "He has scaled the mountains of ignorance. He is about to conquer the highest peak. As he pulls himself over the final rock, he is greeted by a band of theologians who have been sitting there for centuries."

It is true that Christians have believed in heart for centuries. And most still do. I fear that only those of us who are interested in scientific theories have deserted the band sitting on top of the mountain. In this book I hope to encourage those who still sit there, and perhaps call back a few who are climbing up the long way.

In the next chapter I will show how this body-soul question relates to learning. Then in the following chapters I will describe a learning theory which includes heart and other biblical principles.

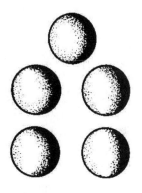

2

Body, Soul, and Learning Theory

Where can we learn about man and his psyche? One obvious place to look is within ourselves. Another source is scientific research on humans. And we can even admit the research on animals to a little space in our psychology, as there are a few similarities between us.

Secular psychologies use those three sources of knowledge, but not necessarily all together. Some feel that introspective self-knowledge is not legitimate for science. Some scoff at the animal research in psychology. Abraham Maslow, for instance, thought so little of it that he felt it was not even worth his time to write a refutation.

As Christians, we can use any and all of these sources. It is right to learn from God's creation. But we can learn from the Creator, too. He has told us much about mankind in the Bible. This, perhaps, is the best source of all.

A biblical psychology ought to be superior to secular

psychology, then. We have the revelation from God, and we can pick the best from scientific studies. We no doubt would be farther along in our science if we based our scientific research on biblical principles.

We can see that with the topic of punishment. Behaviorists, studying how reward and punishment affected the learning of rats, developed the theory that punishment was not effective. There was much writing and teaching about this theory. But then someone tried using a stronger punishment and concluded it was effective. The detour and wasted time could have been saved if the researchers had first learned God's view of punishment, from the Bible. Then they could have spent their time researching how and when to use it for best results, rather than whether to use it.

That is a rather superficial illustration, but it serves to make the point quickly. At a more complex level, a researcher who begins with the Bible would see that God used punishment when the people's hearts were turned against Him. This kind of heart matter cannot even be touched by counting how many times a rat pushes a lever. There is no connection. When the rat principles are applied to a child learning his history there is too loose a fit. Rewards help some. Punishment helps less—at that point of learning. A biblical view of punishment shows that a child needs it when he is rebellious, "foolish," and other attitudes of heart, not when he fails some cognitive task.

So the rat psychologies have no way of getting to the heart of the matter. (Read that either figuratively or literally.) Similar arguments can be shown in relation to humanist psychologies, even though a great deal more of their research may be useful to us. The limitations of these psychologies are built in. They stem from the inadequate view of humans they start with, and from the inadequate sources of their information. This is shown on the chart, Figure 1.

Learning Theory	View of man	Developed from the study of . . .
Behaviorism	personless body	laboratory animals
Humanism	biological organism	people
Biblical	image of God	animals, people, and the Bible

Figure 1. The Bases of Learning Theories

Behaviorist Theories. The first group of theories on the chart are called behaviorist. This includes theories which say that learning comes by conditioning, association and reinforcement. Newer versions are the information processing theories. These use computers instead of rats as models for studying human learning. The human machine may be more complex in these theories, but it is still a machine.

The next space on the chart indicates this view. Man is seen as a personless body. This is not an epithet given by enemies of behaviorism, trying to ridicule the system. It comes directly from the high priest of American behaviorism, B.F. Skinner. Here are his words: "The picture which emerges from a scientific analysis is not of a body with a person inside, but of a body which is a person in the sense that it displays a complex repertoire of behavior. . . . Autonomous man is a device used to explain what we cannot explain in any other way. He has been constructed from our ignorance, and as our understanding increases, the very stuff of which he is composed vanishes" (*Beyond Freedom and Dignity*. New York: Knopf, 1971, pp. 199,200).

In other words, we are superstitious. When people were ignorant about thunder they made up their own explanation and taught children it was the footfall of Zeus. We are smarter about that now. We have been taught a physical explanation for thunder, so we have dropped our superstitious belief in the "personality" behind it. Skinner was saying the same thing will happen to human personality. We will drop our superstitious belief in it when we become as smart as he.

And that will be progress. When we no longer exclaim with Hamlet, "How like a god!" but agree with Pavlov, "How like a dog," it will be a step forward (ibid. p.201).

Behaviorism did not begin with Ivan Pavlov or any other scientist of modern times. Its techniques go far back in history and it was developed to a high level in the falconry of medieval times. This fascinating occupation will make a more interesting description of how behaviorism works than will the story of a laboratory pigeon, so we will use it here.

A young female falcon was caught from wherever the nobleman thought the best falcons were bred. She was put into the darkness of a mews—a falcon roosting house—and her eyes were covered with a hood. Sometimes her eyes were sewn shut. The falconer could not have her both seeing and hearing, as the system called for only one bit of learning at a time. The first learning was to roost on the trainer's wrist (covered with a heavy glove). The falcon was gently carried about the darkened room for a day and a night. On the second day the hungry bird was fed a chicken leg while the falconer stroked her and talked or sang to her. Always when she ate, it was accompanied by the stroking and by her particular call notes. This is classical conditioning, where the associations are together in time; the stroking and eating occur together.

The falcon's eyes were first unsealed in darkness and she was very gradually exposed to light. She was "weathered" to the world outside the mews by roosting on a block nearby. New learnings, such as this, could now be accompanied by stroking or calling instead of by food, because these by now were conditioned stimuli. They would quiet her as the unconditioned stimulus—food—formerly did.

All during this training the falcon was tied with leather "jesses." When she felt at home on her trainer's wrist outdoors, she was taken on horseback. Later she was taught to return to the master by use of the call notes and food. This is operant conditioning, where the desired action is followed by reward: she returned, then she received food. The call notes, always associated with the food, could later be used alone. At this point the jesses were removed and the falcon was allowed to fly free.

This training continued through several steps of working with lures. If the "behavioral objective" was that she would hunt cranes, the lure was made of a crane's wings attached to a piece of meat. At last she became a hunter and valuable property for the king or nobleman who owned her. She might even sleep in her master's bedroom.

The falcon's mystique has gained her a place in mythology, but she still has only a bird brain. And her training admirably fits a bird brain.

This is the system behaviorists would have us use on our children, not only for potty training, but for higher learning, too. In fact, whether we choose it or not, this is the way we learn, they say. It's our environment—the stimuli and rewards—that have shaped us to what we are. Accidental or planned, that's the way it works. The food and call notes, or whatever their equivalent might be in our lives, being associated together, cause certain neural chains to be linked together in the brain—a unit of learning, by classical conditioning. The food as a reward following a behavior causes linkages to the pleasure center of the brain—a bit of learning by operant conditioning. It works negatively, too, by linkage with the punishment center of the brain.

In the bird and in the human there is no person inside to affect learning or behavior. There is no mind or heart to control in any way. Belief in something beyond the body is just like belief in God. Such ideas are only superstitions and will fade away as our scientific understanding grows.

Lenin realized how great an ally he had in this system of thought. It would help in his struggle against religion. So in his time, Pavlov's behaviorism became the official Soviet view of psychology. The English speaking world followed. In America, John Watson was the first great behaviorist. He was both philosopher and psychologist, and felt that concepts such as morality and justice were merely superstitions left over from a pre-scientific age. They would fade away when we learned how like a machine—or a bird—man is. Watson's counterpart in England was Ernest Jones, a follower of Freud. Jones thought that any hope of future evolutionary progress rested on whether man could give up belief in mind.

So with behaviorism has traveled atheism, amorality, and evolution. It's no wonder that so many Christians distrust it.

But the falcon did learn. There is a technique here that has its uses, limited though they may be with humans. Probably the best thing we have gained from behaviorists is the more tested way we now break difficult learning down into small bits and place it in careful order. Also, on a first level learning (as we will be calling it in this book) association and conditioning are helpful concepts to use.

A more recent outgrowth of behaviorism is called "cognitive" theory. This happened when behaviorists got tired of studying tiny bits of learning that could immediately be rewarded or punished. They could not reach their goal of having 11-year-olds become Ph.D.s by just inputting enough of the little bits of learning. So they moved up a level and studied how to teach larger, more meaningful units of learning. But their view of the child as a machine, and all the other views of behaviorism continued with the cognitivists the same as with the behaviorists.

Humanist Theories. On the Figure 1 chart, the second group of theories is called humanist. Lumped together in this group are all the theories which see man as more than a machine or personless body. These theories see him as a biological organism, highest on the evolutionary scale. We group here the theories built on cognitive development and psychological development of people. We include phenomenology which emphasizes the individual's subjective view of his world. We include, also, the Gestalt theories which consider insight to be important. These all emphasize the human. They have been developed by studying people rather than animals.

Gestaltists are called by that German word because there is no English word to say "wholes" in quite the same way. These people talk about the "whole child" and about the "whole field" of learning. They reacted against the behaviorists who atomized learning into such tiny particles, and they tried to put more meaning into learning. They have had an influence which is still with us in our educational thinking. Phenomenology has not had great influence to date.

Of greatest influence today are the developmentalists. These are concerned about the developing human. They study what the child (and adult) is like at different periods in his growth. And they study how he moves from one stage into the next.

Jean Piaget is probably the best known of these. Piaget's monumental studies began influencing education in his lifetime, and no doubt will influence it for a long time to come if the world has a long time left to it. Abraham Maslow's hierarchy of psychological needs, Erik Erikson's stages of life, and Robert Havighurst's developmental tasks all have had considerable influence, too, and probably will continue to do so.

These men all studied humans, not rats. And they studied normal healthy humans, not psychopathic cases, for developing the formulations mentioned here. Each man looked at the human from a different angle and tried to organize what he saw. As an artist helps us see the landscape in a new way, so these have given their varying views of man, helping us to see things perhaps in a new way.

"Oh, but that's humanism!" some are going to exclaim. They are right that the formulations of Piaget, for instance, can be used for a humanist education, but they don't have to be. The trouble comes if we raise the humanist view to a guiding philosophy. For example, if we use Piaget's stages of mental growth as our definition of the child and what his education should be, then our education becomes humanist.

This may be difficult for Christians to understand, because we are so used to thinking of children as God's creatures, with souls, with eternal life ahead, and other supernatural attributes. But try for a moment to shed all this supernatural. Think of a child as the humanist does. He is an animal. A human animal, higher than all others. He arrived by chance in his turn in the evolutionary process, and when he dies that is the end of him. Now if we want to educate the child and bring him to his greatest potential mentally, what will we do? We will study mental development of humans. Then we will arrange our education to lead the child as far along that path as we can. That is bringing him to the greatest potential we know. What more can we do?

Now in practice, a humanist education is not so barren as that. The one-track mental development is used here to keep the illustration simple. There are many kinds of humanists, of course, and most would enrich their education with art, culture, psychological growth, physical training, and so forth. The goal is to make the best human the humanist knows.

The flaw in all this for the Christian is that the humanist knows nothing about the human spirit. The Christian has another dimension in his view of the human. So he has another dimension in his education. He has a far richer education, but he need not throw out everything that humanists might use.

27

Biblical Theory. In formulating a biblical theory of learning we can use all the sources of information that behaviorists and humanists use. The second column of the chart shows that. In addition, we have the Bible. This message from the Creator to the humans He created teaches about the spiritual dimension. It is our best source of information about the immaterial part of man.

What does the immaterial have to do with learning? Can we find out in the Bible? We will pursue these questions in the next chapter.

3

The Immaterial Heart

Writing in 1855, theologian Franz Delitzsch examined the Bible to answer the question of heart *(A System of Biblical Psychology*, first published in 1855, reprinted in English in 1977 by Baker Book House, Grand Rapids). Since the Bible uses the word heart almost 1000 times, that seems a good place to look. Delitzsch came to the conclusion that Scripture attributes a central place to heart in spirit-soul activities and affections. Head and brain may be the noblest part of man and stand in close relation to soul and spirit. But heart is central.

The great scientists of ancient cultures, both in the West and in the Orient, held this view. Hippocrates, the father of modern medicine, did not attribute any soul functions to the brain. Aristotle viewed heart as the central organ of the soul. Scripture, too, has this view. Only the book of Daniel places any spirit-soul events in the head. In Daniel, visions are in the head. But even here is a hint that that is not the whole explanation. Daniel talked to the king about the visions in his head, and in the same conversation called them the thoughts of his heart (Daniel 2:28,30).

From medieval times onward, the scientific view has been different, and the higher functions are no longer attributed to heart. So Delitzsch's conclusions were contrary to his times, as they are to ours. If we give heart the place the ancient cultures and the Scriptures gave it, we are likely to be viewed as those who believe the earth is flat. Nevertheless, I will use a chapter to consider heart as closely related to the spiritual. There are some provocative ideas here and we will be much poorer if we miss them.

Delitzsch wrestled with the implications of his study. It was clear to him what Scripture said about the centrality of heart. (Some of the verses are listed later in this chapter.) But he also was not ignorant about science, medicine, and contemporary thought. In the 1800s it was probably just as difficult as it would be now to figure out how the soul-man is manifested in the flesh-man, keeping Bible-believing Christians happy on one hand and keeping the scientifically informed from scoffing on the other hand. I doubt whether he actually worried about scoffers, yet the scientific problem existed, as it does for us. In this situation, Delitzsch came up with a remarkable statement. I will not quote his full 175-word sentence here, but will try to paraphrase the main idea.

It goes something like this: If it can be proved that the heart and brain "talk" to each other, that would explain the spiritual importance that Scripture gives to heart. He had in mind the nervous character of the heart rather than its muscular character. His idea was that an impression could begin in the brain, which would stimulate the heart. The heart, in turn, would react upon the brain, adding emotion to the impression. From brain, to heart, to brain (pp. 306, 307). He thought this provided only a partial explanation because it accounted only for emotion and not for will and thought, which are also attributed to heart in Scripture.

I call that a remarkable statement because now—about

150 years later—science may be on the verge of agreeing with this scenario. The Laceys, the husband and wife team mentioned in chapter 1, have studied the importance of heart in behavior. They have shown, for one, that the heart goes its own way and does not always respond together with other body reactions. Others have suspected that this is the case, and now experimental research has demonstrated it. This is rather startling in the medical world because the standard belief has been that blood pressure, heart rate, sweating and other indicators of emotion are turned up or down together by a part of the autonomic nervous system. But the Laceys have obtained results contrary to this belief. In their research, when a person needs to give attention to something outside himself his heart rate and blood pressure decrease. When he needs to shut out distractions, they increase. And this heart change is entirely independent of the other indicators of emotion that supposedly react together at the instruction of the autonomic nervous system.

This general result is obtained over a variety of experiments. Taken together, they seem to show the heart "talking" to the brain. The heart in effect says, "Get ready, brain. I've got some hard thinking for you to do." It sends that message by speeding up, not after the brain is hard at work and telling the heart to help it, but before. It happens quickly, within the cycle of one heartbeat.

Another message is, "Watch, brain. You have to be ready to act when the light flashes." The heart sends that message by slowing down its rate and decreasing the blood pressure, again, within the cycle of one heartbeat. This prepares the brain for the job of attending to the light. Brain will "see" the red light and respond to it faster than it could without the heart's help.

When the heart speeds up or slows down, the blood pressure changes accordingly. The nerve endings in the artery walls sense the change and relay the message to the brain. The degree of heart change varies with the person's motivation. If he is more highly motivated there is more change.

The first kind of message—the speeding up—prepares the brain for internal activities. Some activities that the Laceys used in their experiments were figuring out words that were spelled in reverse order, doing mental arithmetic, and making up certain kinds of sentences. For this work the brain needs to shut out distractions in the environment. It doesn't want the body senses picking up sights and sounds. The second kind of message—the slowing down—prepares the brain to receive information through the senses.

You may be wondering if the subjects possibly held their breath or changed breathing in some way that would change heart rate. The Laceys wondered about that too, so they tested and found that breathing had nothing to do with it. They also tested the sweating and other indicators of the autonomic nervous system and found they had nothing to do with the heart change, either. In other words, the traditional view that brain sees the red light and the autonomic nervous system responds as a unit simply does not hold up in these researches. Other research also has been breaking down this textbook view of the autonomic nervous system so that more and more scientists are beginning to doubt it.

This exciting research may be the first crack in what could become a new view of things. At least it admits the possibility that physically the heart does have something to do with motivation, will, and learning, and that the Bible was using the right word all through the years we were making excuses for it.

The Bible's references to heart show that it has far more work to do than just pumping blood. Delitzsch organized the references into three categories—physical, spirit-soul, and moral. That may be appropriate for theologians.

But in this book about learning, I break them down into more categories than that, while still acknowledging my great debt to Delitzsch for this work. These categories follow.

Physical Life. Heart is used only a very few times in its material sense. Abraham and an unnamed man both offered a "morsel of bread" to a guest so that they might strengthen their hearts (Genesis 18:5 and Judges 19:5). David and Solomon wrote of heart as central to life and strength. "My heart panteth, my strength faileth me" (Psalm 38:10). "A sound heart is the life of the flesh" (Proverbs 14:30).

Spiritual Life. After telling the parable of the sower, Jesus explained that the seed was the word of the kingdom and that the field where it was sown was the heart. "When any one heareth the word of the kingdom, and understandeth it not, then cometh the wicked one, and catcheth away that which was sown in his heart" (Matthew 13:39). That verse implies, also, that understanding or lack of it are in the heart.

Belief is in the heart, too. And unbelief. "With the heart man believeth unto righteousness" (Romans 10:10). "Take heed, brethren, lest there be in any of you an evil heart of unbelief, in departing from the living God" (Hebrews 3:12).

Heart decisions can bring a person's heart under the control of God or of Satan. Titus let God use his heart. Ananias, on at least one occasion, let Satan use his. "But thanks be to God, which put the same earnest care into the heart of Titus for you" (II Corinthians 8:16). "Peter said, Ananias, why hath Satan filled thine heart to lie to the Holy Ghost, and to keep back part of the price of the land?" (Acts 5:3).

In the heart of the Christian dwells Christ, the Holy

Spirit, peace, love of God, and heavenly light.

> *That Christ may dwell in your hearts* (Ephesians 3:17).

> [God] *hath also sealed us, and given the earnest of the Spirit in our hearts* (II Corinthians 1:22).

> *Let the peace of God rule in your hearts* (Colossians 3:15).

> *The love of God is shed abroad in our hearts* (Romans 5:5).

> *For God, who commanded the light to shine out of darkness, hath shined in our hearts, to give the light of the knowledge of the glory of God in the face of Jesus Christ* (II Corinthians 4:6).

Moral Life. "The work of the law [is] written in their hearts, their conscience also bearing witness" (Romans 2:15). With the law, comes knowledge of good and evil. Some hearts bring forth the one and some the other.

> *Out of the abundance of the heart the mouth speaketh. A good man out of the good treasure of the heart bringeth forth good things: and an evil man out of the evil treasure bringeth forth evil things* (Matthew 12:34,35).

> *For from within, out of the heart of men, proceed evil thoughts, adulteries, fornications, murders, thefts, covetousness, wickedness, deceit, lasciviousness, an evil eye, blasphemy, pride, foolishness* (Mark 7:21,22).

Having capacity for good or evil, the heart is said in Scripture to be pure, upright, whole, perfect, strong, faithful, and all their opposites. Here are a few verses mentioning the good.

> *He that loveth pureness of heart, for the grace of his lips the king shall be his friend* (Proverbs 22:11).

> *Shout for joy, all ye that are upright in heart* (Psalm 32:11).

> *Let your heart therefore be perfect with the LORD our God, to walk in his statutes, and to keep his commandments* (I Kings 8:61).

Here is the opposite.

> *And ye have done worse than your father; for, behold, ye walk every one after the imagination of his evil heart, that they may not hearken unto me* (Jeremiah 16:12).

The good and the evil mentioned in these verses come from the heart, but it is a heart that knows which is which, because the law is written there. Therefore the heart must be the seat of conscience. We find that indication in Hebrews 10:22. "Let us draw near with a true heart in full assurance of faith, having our hearts sprinkled from an evil conscience." I will have more to say about conscience in a later chapter. It is important in learning theory.

The heart either loves God or it is lifted in pride against Him.

> *Thine heart is lifted up, and thou hast said, I am a God, I sit in the seat of God, in the midst of the seas; yet thou art a man, and not God, though thou set thine heart as the heart of God. . . . Thine heart is lifted up because of thy riches* (Ezekiel 28:2,5).

Thou shalt love the LORD *thy God with all thy heart, and with all thy soul, and with all thy mind* (Matthew 22:37).

Incidentally, this last verse indicates that heart is not a synonym for mind, since both are mentioned. A heart turned from God is darkened or hardened. But when it turns to God, it is light again.

Because that, when they knew God, they glorified him not as God, neither were thankful; but became vain in their imaginations, and their foolish heart was darkened (Romans 1:21).

O LORD, *why hast thou made us to err from thy ways, and hardened our heart from thy fear?* (Isaiah 63:17).

Even unto this day, when Moses is read, the vail is upon their heart. Nevertheless, when it shall turn to the LORD, *the vail shall be taken away* (II Corinthians 3:15,16).

Emotional Life. The heart loves and hates. It rejoices and sorrows. It holds anger, despair, fear, sympathy. Here is a representative sampling of the numerous verses in this category.

Now the end of the commandment is charity [love] *out of a pure heart* (I Timothy 1:5).

Thou shalt not hate thy brother in thine heart (Leviticus 19:17).

My servants shall sing for joy of heart, but ye shall cry for sorrow of heart (Isaiah 65:14).

They . . . did eat their meat with gladness and

singleness of heart (Acts 2:46).

As he that taketh away a garment in cold weather . . . so is he that singeth songs to an heavy heart (Proverbs 25:20).

Because I have said these things unto you, sorrow hath filled your heart (John 16:6).

For I am poor and needy, and my heart is wounded within me (Psalm 109:22).

When they heard these things, they were cut to the heart, and they gnashed on him with their teeth (Acts 7:54).

Lest the avenger of blood pursue the slayer, while his heart is hot . . . (Deuteronomy 19:6).

Therefore I went about to cause my heart to despair of all the labour which I took under the sun (Ecclesiastes 2:20).

I [God] *will put my fear in their hearts, that they shall not depart from me* (Jeremiah 32:40).

The LORD *shall smite thee with madness, and blindness, and astonishment of heart*
(Deuteronomy 28:28).

My heart within me is desolate (Psalm 143:4).

When all the kings . . . heard that the LORD *had dried up the waters of Jordan from before the children of Israel, until we were passed over, that their heart melted, neither was there spirit in them any more:* (Joshua 5:1).

Emotions are in God's heart too. "How shall I give

thee up, Ephraim? . . . mine heart is turned within me"
(Hosea 11:8).

Motivations. In these categories we have been moving gradually from what is considered more spiritual or
religious to the more psychological. Good and evil, belief
and unbelief, loving and hating—these all come from the
heart, according to Scripture. Now, what about motivation?
Motivation is important in many learning theories. And it
is important in the biblical theory which is presented in the
next chapter.

Solomon was motivated to learn. "I gave my heart to
seek and search out by wisdom concerning all things that
are done under heaven" (Ecclesiastes 1:13).

Others were motivated to do either evil or good. If
our current education on drugs, sex, and such things took
account of heart instead of just head information it would
likely be more successful. These Bible people determined,
desired, or willed to do either good or evil:

> *The children of Israel brought a willing offer-
> ing unto the LORD, every man and woman, whose
> heart made them willing* (Exodus 35:29).

> *Daniel purposed in his heart that he would
> not defile himself with the portion of the king's
> meat* (Daniel 1:8).

> *Who is he . . . that durst presume in his heart
> to do so?* (Esther 7:5).

> *Because sentence against evil work is not ex-
> ecuted speedily, therefore the heart of the sons
> of men is fully set in them to do evil* (Ecclesiastes
> 8:11).

Thought Life. Even thoughts are not left only to the
head. In the verses quoted below we see that the heart

perceives. Then it knows, understands, and speaks through the mouth out of this knowledge.

Yet the LORD *hath not given you an heart to perceive, and eyes to see, and ears to hear, unto this day* (Deuteronomy 29:4).

When Jesus rules, *The heart also of the rash shall understand knowledge* (Isaiah 32:4).

In our times, "Wisdom resteth in the heart of him that hath understanding.... The lips of the wise disperse knowledge: but the heart of the foolish doeth not so.... The heart of him that hath understanding seeketh knowledge: but the mouth of fools feedeth on foolishness.... The heart of the righteous studieth to answer: but the mouth of the wicked poureth out evil things.... The wise in heart shall be called prudent: and the sweetness of the lips increaseth learning.... The heart of the wise teacheth his mouth and addeth to his lips" (Proverbs 14:33; 15:7,14,28; 16:21,23).

When Elisha wanted to tell Gehazi that he knew of his secret dishonesty, he said it this way: "Went not mine heart with thee?" (II Kings 5:26).

Joshua said, "Ye know in all your hearts and in all your souls, that not one thing hath failed of all the good things which the LORD your God spake concerning you" (Joshua 23:14).

Not only does the heart know things; it also considers, ponders, and meditates upon them.

Consider in thine heart: (Deuteronomy 8:5).

Mary kept all these things, and pondered them in her heart: (Luke 2:19).

Let the words of my mouth, and the meditation of my heart, be acceptable in thy sight, O

LORD, my strength, and my redeemer (Psalm 19:14).

Knowledge of God's Word is stored in the heart.

Lay up these words in your heart and in your soul (Deuteronomy 11:18).

Bind them continually upon thine heart (Proverbs 6:21).

And all they that heard them [sayings] *laid them up in their hearts* (Luke 1:66).

An inner discourse seems to take place in the heart. "Abraham . . . said in his heart" (Genesis 8:21). "When thou saidst, Seek ye my face; my heart said unto thee, Thy face, LORD, will I seek" (Psalm 27:8). The "thoughts" of someone's heart are mentioned in Genesis 6:5, Daniel 2:30 and elsewhere.

The above verses give some samples of what the heart does according to the Bible. Appendix A gives a complete list of all 981 uses of *heart* in the Bible. Amazingly, the dominant category is "thought." These usages total 24.8%, whereas the physical heart is meant just 1.6% of the time. Other high categories are moral at 21.7%, emotion at 17.9% and spiritual at 14.3%. So the real heart, according to the Bible is not just a blood pump.

Science has been relatively silent about the role of heart in the soul matters of thoughts, motivations, and so forth. Few are even researching in this direction. But some people, besides the Laceys, are pursuing this scientifically. (More on this in a later chapter.)

Former times saw more interest in this question. When King Charles II of Spanish Inquisition infamy died in 1700, there was evidently an autopsy performed and it was reported that his heart was not larger than a pigeon's egg, and as soft as moistened chalk. Investigations of the hearts of people who had had melancholy and mania showed defects of the heart without accompanying defects of the brain (Delitzsch, page 305). Presumably these refer to gross physical defects, as men in those days did not have our modern knowledge of RNA molecules and such things to check into.

It is quite acceptable in our times to associate mind with brain, to assume that immaterial mind works through us by using our material brain. It is less acceptable to associate heart with heart, to assume that the age-old immaterial heart functions work through us by using our material heart. Time may change that.

But the fact remains that the Bible gives great prominence to heart, and a biblical learning theory cannot ignore that. Throughout the rest of this book I will use the biblical word heart. The next chapter presents, in brief, the basic form of a biblical learning model. It gives place to heart as well as head.

4

A Model of Learning

Learning theory is exciting. People working in other fields may laugh at that, but I am sure a good many educators reading this know exactly what I mean.

I recall when I was learning about behavioral objectives and the accompanying system of writing programmed learning, I received an A on my program for teaching a certain phonetic spelling rule. That was fun and easy, and furthermore it was Scientific, spelled with a capital S. We at last had learned how people learn. I could make a career of writing programs for the budding new teaching machine industry. And think what I could do for education that way!

The pigeons and the rats bothered me, but I hadn't figured out very well what was wrong. I kept trying to talk about will, but the professor pooh-poohed that and no one else in the class seemed to be interested in will. We were all being Scientific, and that's where the action was in those days.

The class met on Tuesday evenings and, fortunately

for me, I had to meet my class of real, live seventh graders again each Wednesday morning. They helped me keep my feet on the ground. Sweet, doll-like Sally, with a low IQ, filled a notebook with exquisite drawings of Early American furniture for one of our history units. For our study of city life and problems, Robert, a Jew, chose a city that had recently been in the news because of race problems. He wrote to a newspaper in that city and received replies from several thoughtful citizens. All of us learned some things the newspapers had not told us. Sydney, a budding photographer and humorist, took pictures of his classmates and arranged them on a bulletin board with clever and often hilarious captions. Jerry, a math whiz, devoured the books I gave him on mental arithmetic, shortcuts, and tricky math to mystify his friends. From time to time he prepared a demonstration and mystified us. There's nothing like a living classroom to convince you that science does not yet, and probably never will, have *The System* for learning.

In the years since then, mountains of programmed books have been published and I have used some—particularly the ones for beginning reading. I found them useful with certain children, and I have taught hundreds of children with reading problems, using those books as part of my teaching approach. So I give the behaviorists credit for adding to our teaching tools. But I continue to think of students as people with much control over their own learning. I am not a behaviorist shaping them from the outside. Their learning is inside and I am a fellow human trying to help them along the learning road.

I have watched in others this initial excitement or conviction about a learning theory, and then the fading. A seminary professor had run across behavioral objectives. With the enthusiasm of a powerful personality he was ready to write a book about how to teach. My timid personality was no match for his, so I did not debate theory. I tried asking a question instead.

"Do you use behavioral objectives in your education class?"

"Well, I'm going to. I'm going to break my course down into a behavioral objective for every class session."

"I'd like to see how that works out." In my heart I knew he would talk differently in about two years. Many years have passed and his system never materialized. Neither did the book.

A reading specialist had the same enthusiasm when she was taking a graduate course in behaviorist techniques. Armed with M&Ms, counters, and so forth, she overhauled her remedial reading sessions. She told me all the things she was going to do. When I saw her a couple of years later, I asked, "Are you still using behaviorism?"

"No, I dropped that and tried transaction analysis. Later I dropped that, too. Now I just use what I want to from all the theories."

In my hobby of theory watching, I find a different situation exists with needs theory—that which says all learning is to fulfill a need, drive, or hunger, as they have been variously called. I do not find people who have tried it and dropped it. I find many people who assume that needs are the "cause" of learning, but then I find a wide variation in how they define needs. If almost anything can be called a need, then teachers may be right that needs are behind learning. A good many people really mean, "I think they need to learn this, so this is what I teach them." For example, one professor said, "Well if a church is in a cult area, then the people need doctrinal teaching." Others use needs as interest arousers: "I find it easy to teach to a child's needs. For instance, I talk about being thirsty, and then I give the story of Ishmael in the desert."

Needs theory does not change teaching styles quite like behaviorism does, but it affects content. The recent rash of courses and teaching materials designed to build self-image is a result of Maslow's pyramid of needs, which includes self-esteem needs.

I see needs theory, and the older "drive" theories, as a sort of word game we all play. To play this game you begin by observing what humans do. You see that people drink water: Ergo! they have a need for water. Now just reverse your moves and you can explain man's behavior. Why does he drink water? Because he has a "need" for water, of course.

Try it with love, sex, achievement, self-actualizing. It is a great game. You can win every time.

The excitement in a learning theory comes from the feeling that maybe now—at last—we are at the root of the matter. If we know how people learn we can plan our teaching just right, and students will learn better than ever before.

The fading comes when we begin to see we were wrong. People prove bigger than our theories. Somehow Moses learned. And Daniel and Paul. Also the Aristotles and Homers of secular tradition. God did not leave mankind floundering with a half-used brain until our modern science came along to figure out how we should use it.

Modern research and theories do give various views of man and his learning, but the Bible gives the "soul" view. And that is too important to omit from a learning theory. The model of learning presented here uses Bible information and research information, too, where it fits.

The form of the model is from John A.R. Wilson and Mildred D. Robeck, educational psychologists who wanted a model which allowed for more complexity in learning than existing ones. They presented their model in a textbook they co-authored, along with William B. Michael, called *Psychological Foundations of Learning* (New York: McGraw Hill, 1969).

To attain some of the complexity needed, their model included both cognitive learning and motivation learning, with three levels of each. That is the form I use here: three levels and two sides, with a merging of the two at the top level. See Figure 2. This form has proved quite workable for setting down a biblical theory of learning, so I use it, but I change some of the labels and interactions among the parts. We will now look briefly at each of the parts.

Parental Love and Discipline. Discipline is the beginning point. At the lower right, the model shows parental love and discipline, and all arrows move outward from there.

Why does learning begin with discipline? In both Psalms and Proverbs we read that the fear of the Lord is the beginning of wisdom and of knowledge. So how does a child reach the point of fearing the Lord? By the father's discipline, which teaches him to fear his father. A child too young to be told about the Lord can learn fear through loving discipline. "For whom the LORD loveth he correcteth; even as a father the son in whom he delighteth. . . . A rod is for the back of him who is void of understanding" (Proverbs 3:12; 10:13). The father disciplines and when the child is older he comes to see God as he earlier saw his father. And he fears God. This is the beginning of learning.

Fear is an unpopular word to use in our day, and if some prefer to use the word respect, it still comes out the same. Children who are disciplined learn respect for their parents and teachers. And that respect can be transferred to God.

Bruno Bettelheim, a child psychiatrist, wrote about fear and learning. Though he cautioned against a crippling fear, he wrote that "while conscience originates in fear, any

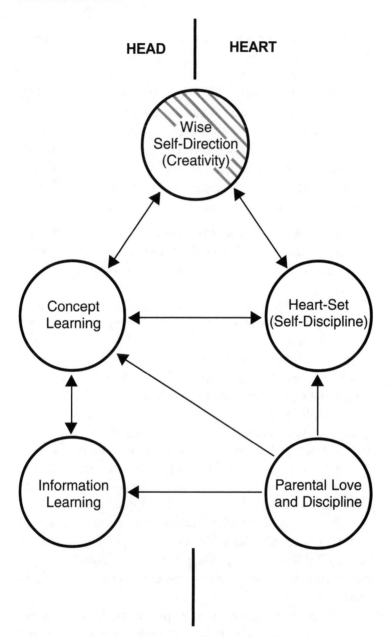

Figure 2. Learning Model

learning that is not immediately enjoyable depends on the prior formation of a conscience" *(Surviving and Other Essays.* New York: Knopf, 1979, p. 130).

Thus there may be a little learning by the "pleasure principle," but that does not go very far. For any significant learning, a person must operate by the "reality principle" in which rewards are delayed. And for that he needs conscience. So Bettelheim teaches this order:

      1) fear
      2) conscience
      3) learning.

He does not advocate basing academic learning on fear directly. "But the child must fear something if he is to apply himself to the arduous task of learning. My contention is that for education to proceed, children must have learned to fear something before they come to school. If it is not the fear of damnation and the woodshed, then in our more enlightened days it must be at least the fear of losing parental love and respect (or later, by proxy, the teacher's) and eventually, the fear of losing self-respect" (ibid., p.133). This comes from a leading child psychiatrist, who wrote a number of helpful things from his non-Christian viewpoint.

Christian teaching, which includes hell as well as heaven, and which includes an all-powerful God, continues to instill the old-fashioned fears. A large part of the superiority of a good Christian school stems from this. Children in such a school come mostly from homes where the fear of God has been instilled in them. So they bring to school an ability to apply themselves to the work of learning. And, of course, homeschooling families benefit directly from these old-fashioned fears without even the proxy of a teacher to filter them.

When parents discipline they are really teaching, according to the Greek word *paiduo.*

No English word is quite like this. Sometimes it is translated as learn, teach, or instruct, and other times translated as chasten.

Can teaching be chastening or chastening be teaching? In this word it is. To see better what this might mean, let's switch the translations around in several familiar verses. Let's say *teach* where the English says *chasten* and vice versa. Remember, it's all the same word. Here are the results:

> *And Moses was chastened in all the wisdom of the Egyptians* (Acts 7:22).

> *. . . and* [Paul] *was chastened according to the perfect manner of the law of the fathers* (Acts 22:3).

> *. . . whom the LORD loveth he teacheth . . . for what son is he whom the father teacheth not?* (Hebrews 12:6,7).

Our word *learn* formerly was used to mean both learn and teach. At one time a parent might have said in threatening tones, "I'll learn you." And I suppose some still do.

When parents have done their chastening-teaching job well, teachers find that children are already motivated to learn. They simply step into the parent's place and continue the teaching process.

In summary, then, learning begins with loving discipline, first from the parents and later, when necessary, from teachers. On the model, arrows point left to learning Levels 1 and 2. These indicate that with discipline a child can learn at these levels. The arrow pointing upward indicates that with imposed discipline a child develops an inner self-discipline.

Heart-Set and Self-Discipline. The growth of self-discipline is gradual. It is an on-again, off-again thing. In

50

some situations and in some matters a child can manage, but in others he still needs the help of parents and teachers imposing discipline from outside himself. All through a child's growing years the adults in his life should keep a proper balance in this. They can allow freedom when the child handles it well. But they should impose structure and discipline when he needs it.

The arrows pointing outward from this part of the model indicate that with self-discipline a person can learn at all levels. The arrows pointing back inward indicate the reciprocal relation—that learning increases discipline. When a person learns, he finds various rewards. Once in a while learning is just plain fun. A person finds immediate pleasure in it. More often he finds some psychological reward—a pride of accomplishment, an increased confidence, or a feeling that he is enriching his life. Sometimes there is not much feeling about it, but simply a knowing that it's worthwhile—either for now or later. These results of learning act as rewards, and make the person more likely to discipline himself for still more learning.

Thus, the learning itself helps to build more self-discipline. It works both ways, as the arrows show. Discipline leads to learning, and learning, in turn, leads to more discipline.

By using the word "reward," I don't intend to say it works by behaviorist principles. Most of the inner rewards we are looking at here are kinds the behaviorists do not have in their system. These are matters of mind and heart. An undisciplined child will seem at times to fit the behaviorist explanation. He lives by the "pleasure principle." We may get him to learn something if we make it fun or immediately rewarding, but this learning can never go very far. It is exhausting for us and it achieves no significant learning in the child.

The more disciplined a child is the more he comes to

live by the reality principle. He can work for delayed rewards—even as far off as heaven. He can work hard because he knows he should, because it's right. This shows
the spiritual aspect of learning; it shows the place of conscience and heart-set.

Heart-set is not determined by conditioning. We teach
and discipline to do what we can for the child's heart and
conscience. But the ultimate choice is his. He determines
which way his heart will be set.

In Psalm 78 we read concerning teaching and heart-
set. The Israelites were to teach their children of God's great
works so their hearts would be right. The psalm goes on to
explain, paradoxically, how much the fathers knew of God's
works, yet their hearts were not right.

The person is inside. We cannot reckon without the
person. We teach, and hopefully most will set their hearts
this way, but some will set their hearts that way. There is
no formula to condition or control a generation of children
in any particular direction.

So on the motivation side of the learning model, heart
is deeply involved. Conscience, will, purpose, and determination, which we saw in Chapter 3 as being associated
with the heart, play their part in learning. They must be
part of a biblical theory of learning.

Information Learning. Level 1 on the left side of the
model is information learning. This is sheer knowing the
stuff. Two plus two is four. Paris is the capital of France,
Paul is known as the first missionary, and so forth. What
we call rote learning belongs here. Association learning is
here—also learning by conditioning or repetition or
memorizing. If we want to use behaviorist techniques in
our teaching we will have to use them mostly for this level
of learning.

Calling this Level 1 learning is not to imply that this kind of learning has low value. It only describes the fact that it is lower in complexity. Value is another matter. A child can learn, for instance, that Jesus died for his sins. This fact has high value. Many facts are important, either by themselves or as part of a larger body of knowledge. Information is essential to any higher learning. Any time we break something down into steps or stages or levels we have a tendency to value the higher ones and devalue the lower ones. But value is a philosophical question. And here we are considering the psychological questions of learning, trying to analyze the process and form a usable model of it. The value of a piece of learning will not necessarily be dependent on its level.

Concept Learning. This level is having insight and understanding beyond the facts of Level 1, seeing relationships among them. Arriving at this level is the "aha" experience. It is the exhilarating experience of moving from Level 1 knowledge of certain facts to a Level 2 understanding of their relationships. The originator of discovery learning, J.R. Suchman, had this experience in mind when he used the word "discovery." But not all who write about discovery learning these days attach the same meaning to the term.

Level 2 learning happens at all ages and with various kinds of learnings. This model is not a "stage" sort of structure, where younger children are at the lower stage, middle-aged ones at the next, and older students on the top stage. A musician may be largely at Level 1 in his learning of space travel, knowing about such things as rockets, shuttles, gravity, and astronomical distances, but with limited insight. In music he will have gained numerous Level 2 concepts. And he may be working creatively at Level 3 on one or more projects. A preschool child may be able to perceive square bead, round bead, square bead, round bead, and copy the pattern correctly on his own string. That is Level 1. After enough experiences of this kind he will understand the concept "pattern" and be able to look for and figure out various kinds of patterns. He will have Level 2 insight into what bead patterns are all about. And one day he may invent a new pattern of his own—Level 3 creativity.

So age or subject matter are not the factors which determine level in this model. What counts is the inner working of the mind.

The arrow between the first and second levels points in both directions. The upward direction is to show that it takes a base of information for the mind to experience conceptualization. The downward direction is to indicate that the concept then reaches down for more facts to fill it. Some reader may say, "Aha, I see the difference between Level 1 and Level 2 learning." Then he will begin noticing in himself or in his pupils various examples of one or the other of those levels. Having the concept now, he will gather in to it more information. It will actually generate more information for him because he now will be aware of things that formerly escaped him.

As time goes on, a concept is adjusted in various ways. New information keeps moving the fences, battering them, or building them stronger. There is continual interplay between Levels 1 and 2.

Wise Self-Direction. Heart-set and learning merge into wisdom. The fear of the Lord was the beginning of this wisdom, and instruction was its growth. "Give instruction to a wise man, and he will be yet wiser: teach a just man, and he will increase in learning" (Proverbs 9:9).

With sufficient self-discipline and a sufficient base of knowledge a person can take charge of his own learning.

He can direct himself. This, again, is not a stage people reach by a certain age. It is a learning process that can happen at all ages. A young child may be creative as he plays with blocks. His previous concepts of blocks and of garages are the knowledge base—the left side of the model. His desire comes from the heart-set or motivation side. Merging these together he can creatively work out the problems of building a garage.

This has been a brief look at the learning model. Chapters 6 to 9 will give a deeper look at various parts of it. But before taking up those parts we will evaluate the model in terms of the science-Bible question. How scientific is it? How biblical is it? And is it what we need?

5

The Science-Bible Question

We all remember from our schoolbooks the legend of Galileo dropping weights from the tower of Pisa. We learned what a breakthrough for science that was, what a turning point in the thinking of Western man. And indeed it was. But while we reap the 400 years of benefits, few notice what we lost. Professor Roger Poole of England has written a book on the loss. He wrote that in "mathematizing" nature, "Galileo shears away the entire world of sense-impressions, emotions, and all the realities that make up our everyday world. Then, he substitutes a knowledge of the mathematical properties of the world, for that complete, total human world that we knew before, and counts himself richer by the exchange" (*Towards Deep Subjectivity*. London: Allen Lane, 1972, p. 82).

Others besides Galileo have advanced this way of thinking, and the dominant trend through these centuries for science and philosophy has been behaviorist, determinist, positivist, and objectivist. The mathematizing came into

57

the field of educational psychology only in the twentieth century, as statistical methods that were first developed for agricultural experiments were appropriated for use in psychological and educational experiments. So we gather our numbers and think we know something when we read them. B. F. Skinner said we can only know what we can measure.

Once with a class on psychological measurements I took a test designed to measure values. One question asked me what I would do with an extra $10. Well, any tithing Christian knows how the tithe comes off first. Then other giving that is on your heart and the necessary bills get paid. After that you can begin to think about "extra" money. The question asked if I would go to a concert with the extra money, or buy a book, or give it to my church. I checked *concert*. Score one for aesthetic value. On a similar question I checked *book*. Score for intellectual value.

When my profile was finished it looked more or less balanced among all the values. A classmate said, "I would have thought yours would be extra high on religious value." This casual acquaintance measured me better than the test did.

At a much earlier time I took an introvert/extrovert test. I was not test-wise in those days. I answered the questions in all earnestness, thinking I would actually learn something about myself. To my surprise and that of my friends, the score came out high on the extrovert side. My bookish ways and lack of gregariousness would not have earned me the label "extrovert," but I was privately pleased. I tried to explain it to my roommate by saying, "Maybe extrovert is really an interest in other people, and whether you show it in loud ways or not is not the main point." I wonder what a test of pride would have shown then. Anyway, I long since have ceased to care what extrovert is, and whether I am one or not.

Poole wrote that the idea of personality as extroverted/ introverted or neurotic/balanced, and so forth has not in fact advanced beyond what the ancients had in their four humors (sanguine, choleric, phlegmatic, melancholy). Even though these are presented with impressive columns of decimalized figures, the ideas are "medieval, not to say astrological, in conceptual primitiveness." The attempt to mathematize such attributes is "the modern equivalent of alchemy" (ibid. p. 54).

Edmund Husserl, a German philosopher known as the founder of phenomenology, wrote, "No objective science, no matter how exact, explains or ever can explain anything in a serious sense" (ibid. p. 95). There is always too much left over.

Phenomenology is a backlash to sterile objectivity. Teachers study it in psychology classes and try to learn the importance of how each individual subjectively sees his world. The thinker is related to the thought. But the movement has fought a losing battle against the forces of objectivity, and the most often used fragment from those classes is the term "tunnel vision." When someone stubbornly refuses to see things as you think he should, you can knowingly explain to your educated friends that he has tunnel vision. This marks you as a member of the education fraternity.

Glasser's reality therapy and Powers' control theory emphasize the inner world of the individual. But even in this form, the inner world as the individual sees it is not the same as the Christian idea of an "inner man" who sees his world.

One who sees man as made in the image of God has little trouble seeing that an inner man should be part of the totality of any situation. The moral and spiritual dimensions, the heart aspects, cannot be left out in trying to describe any "facts" or "truth" about human psychology. The believer in God also sees the idea of objective truth easily. If God created, then His creation "is," and it is there for us to study. We can gain knowledge subjectively. We can also use knowledge that we think we get objectively, although true objectivity may be impossible. And we have a third source in God's revelation, the Bible. The Bible is first in importance. It is the most dependable source of information about ourselves. Our subjective reflections and our "objective" researches should be measured against the Bible. Whatever fits can become part of our biblical learning theory.

To recap our three categories of learning theories here (see page 21), we would say, first, that behaviorists are entirely in the objectivist (scientific) camp. They think they have developed their theory objectively and they think that learning for all of us is only objective; we do not have any inner man who can be subjective.

Second, the humanists may be in either or both of the first two camps. Some specifically denounce objectivism and rely on subjective questionnaires and interviews to study humans. But most, while they may use these techniques, still have a loyalty to objectivism that goes with our post-Galileo times. These often think that their theories are developed quite objectively from their research. But others think that the reverse is true—that research is arranged so as to bear out previously held subjective feelings. This latter may be either a conscious or an unconscious process. Piaget, for instance, claimed that his theories grew out of his observations of infants and children. But at age 19 he wrote a novel of an adolescent's searchings and in that novel can be found the major ideas that he spent his life working out.

Now for our biblical theory, we can claim to be in three camps—objectivist, subjectivist, and "revelationist."

That third dimension—the Bible—opens our eyes to some aspects of learning that would never come by modern science. All theories leak. Whether scientific or not, the nature of theories is that they leak. Theories attempt to describe in a brief way what happens in nature, and nature is always bigger than the description. With the three learning levels, for instance—fact, concept, and creativity—we find them useful as categories. But the real case probably is that there is an infinite continuum from a low, fact level on upward as high as a person can go in this life on the left side of the model, with also an infinite variation in the amount of affect or heart that is mixed in (the right side). But for manageability we draw lines. As we draw lines between child, adolescent and adult in individuals or between lower, middle and upper classes in society, so we draw lines between Levels 1, 2, and 3 of learning.

The real case for any single learning sequence is that it may happen in any of an infinite number of ways. The arrows on the model indicate the various directions it might happen. We will now examine some of these directions more closely.

A common proposition is that learning proceeds from knowledge to application. Schoolteachers usually think of this order strictly in the cognitive realm (left side of the model). For instance, by teaching a child the numbers and certain understandings of them, they expect to bring the child to the place where he can apply his knowledge in working out problems.

In Christian education writings, this order sometimes appears to begin in the cognitive, but then slips over to the heart side when it comes to application. We are told to begin at the "knowing" level—to teach the child what the Bible says. Then we are to move to the "understanding" level—to make sure the child understands what the Bible says.

The words may vary from book to book, but this basic order is used. After understanding, we are to proceed to a "life response" or "life application" level. The learning model indicates that this last level of learning will only happen if both legs are under it. Both the head and the heart have to be involved to achieve the desired life application result. Secular education tries the one-leg approach. And it gets poor results. Teaching about drugs for the head alone does not reduce the use of drugs in life. The same can be said for teaching about sex or morals or any other topic where we hope for more than just a cognitive result. National Assessment testing and 1980 surveys in the United States showed that 90 percent of teenagers considered smoking to be harmful, yet smoking was still increasing among teenagers.

In the biblical view, we would think of a learning sequence as beginning with heart-set rather than beginning with knowledge. Jesus said, "If any man will to do his [Father's] will, he shall know of the doctrine" (John 7:17).

Purpose comes first. Intention of the heart leads to knowledge. One man walked halfway across Asia searching for someone who could tell him about God. It was not the knowledge of God which led to that behavior, but it was purpose of heart which led him eventually to the knowledge. This happens in lesser ways in countless classes. Those with purpose learn.

Psalm 78 shows that order of learning—from heart-set to knowledge, and on to life application of the knowledge. See Figure 3 for a diagram of how this works. God had disciplined the people with anger and with love, as we read throughout the psalm. Those who internalized the discipline could give ear and incline their ears as admonished to do in verse 1. These verbs indicate inner purpose. The learning sequence of Psalm 78 begins here. Heart-set first. This leads to knowing and remembering the

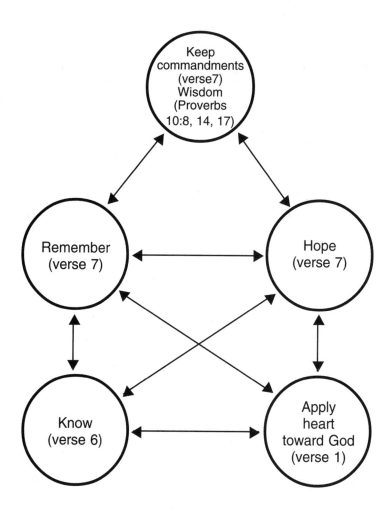

Figure 3. Psalm 78 wisdom learning. Heart-set and knowledge combine to achieve life application results.

commandments. The knowing and the heart attitudes, which now include hope, combine to achieve the wise result of keeping the commandments. Head knowledge alone would not have led there.

In verse 7 we read two objectives for teaching the children—that they might "set their hope in God" and "keep his commandments." This may look at first like a "knowledge to life-application" formula for teaching. But that's only part of the message of this psalm. We see on careful reading that everyone did not reach the objectives. The fathers had the knowledge. God did marvelous works in their sight. He did miracle after miracle. Talk about visual aids—that generation had them more than any generation since. Yet they "kept not the covenant of God, and refused to walk in his law." Why didn't the fathers apply their knowledge? Because their hearts were not right with God.

Actually, the fathers did learn life applications, but all the wrong ones. They lusted, lied, and sinned in many ways. So God in the end gave them over to destruction. This sequence that ends in destruction is foolishness learning, or negative learning. The Psalm 78 example is in the upside-down diagram of the learning model in Figure 4.

So we have a contrast. All the people received the same information. In one group it led to foolishness and destruction. For others, including the psalmist himself, presumably, it led to keeping the commandments, which was wisdom and life.

Why such opposite results from the same teaching? The key is heart-set. The stubborn ones "set not their hearts aright" (verse 8) and "their heart was not right with him (verse 37). This negative heart-set led to speaking against God, forgetting His works, not believing or trusting Him, lusting, flattering, and lying. This is foolishness—the opposite of wisdom. And because of their foolishness God ultimately destroyed them.

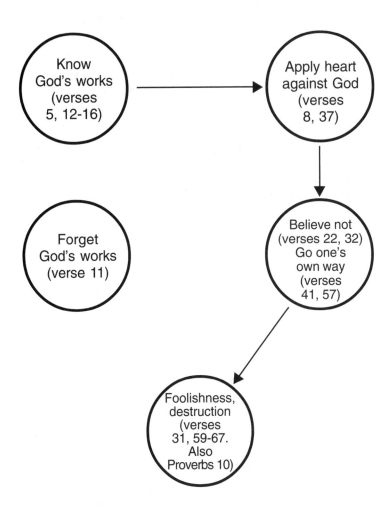

Figure 4. Psalm 78 foolishness learning. Heart set against God leads to destruction.

Many of the proverbs, particularly chapter 10, give this same contrast between wisdom and foolishness. Solomon wrote that receiving the commandments and heeding instruction is wisdom. And it is the way of life. The opposite is foolishness, and it is the way of destruction. These ideas can be diagrammed in ladder form as in Figures 5 and 6. Bettelheim, as we have seen, shows this order for learning, as he argues for the importance of conscience.

These ladders are not meant to propose that we can do a great deal about setting learning in a linear sequence for our students. The ladders are simply insets taken from the total learning model, and if we looked closely at the model we would see thousands of these ladders reaching in all directions, climbing on numerous levels all at once.

Try, for instance, to imagine a child learning the word Jerusalem. When he first meets it, it is likely to mean only a place—perhaps the place were Joseph and Mary brought baby Jesus to the temple. And, of course, the child has nothing like his teacher's idea of Jerusalem in his mind at such a time. It may mean almost nothing to him, but he does hear the word. As time goes on he learns more about Jerusalem: it had a temple in it, walls around it. His concept of city is also growing and he can begin to picture a city of Jerusalem. Pictures help, and more stories of what happened there. He learns of its earlier history, when Joshua conquered it, when David made it his capital. He learns of its destruction. During his teen years he may spend a semester there studying. All through his growing years (which may be his whole life) he gains a continually richer meaning for the word Jerusalem. So while the student may be learning more words, he at the same time is learning more about each word. We might say that his vocabulary grows qualitatively as well as quantitatively.

At what point will we say a student has "mastered" Jerusalem and is ready to go on to the next item? It really is

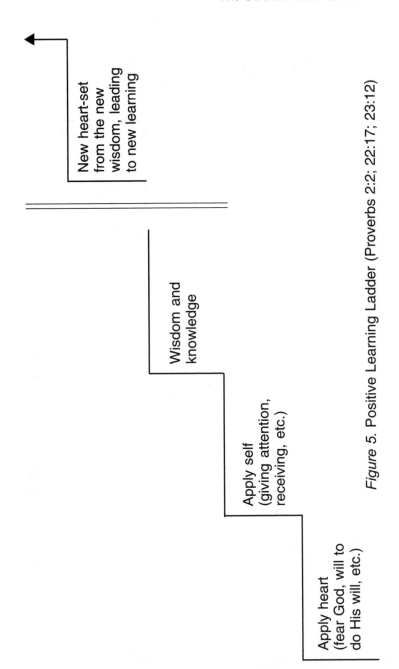

New heart-set from the new wisdom, leading to new learning

Wisdom and knowledge

Apply self (giving attention, receiving, etc.)

Apply heart (fear God, will to do His will, etc.)

Figure 5. Positive Learning Ladder (Proverbs 2:2; 22:17; 23:12)

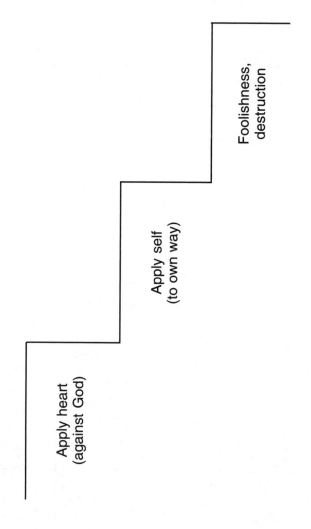

Apply heart
(against God)

Apply self
(to own way)

Foolishness,
destruction

Figure 6. Negative learning ladder (Psalm 78; Proverbs 10)

not possible to be very linear about learning. Piaget, who more than anyone else worked at breaking down children's learning into bits and describing them, came to the conclusion that it is not possible to lay bits out in linear fashion for children to learn. In setting out curriculum content we make considered judgments, and we keep our classes moving along in a general way. But individual students are bursting out all the seams. They do not stay in line.

In short, there is no scientific explanation of learning. Many people have argued that it's a fallacy to call education and psychology sciences. They are not sciences in the sense that physics is. And when they do behave like sciences, they leave out heart and soul, the most important ingredients. So it is right for our theory of learning to draw from the Bible more than from science.

A Bible figure for learning is "growth." Growth happens all over at the same time. Milk and meat are given to help growth along. Children grow like olive plants, which will develop into trees (Psalm 128:3). The righteous shall flourish like the palm tree and grow like the cedar (Psalm 92:2). They shall bear fruit and have green leaves (Psalm 1:3).

The next three chapters explore growth on each of the three levels of the learning model. We will begin with creativity and work our way downward to memory.

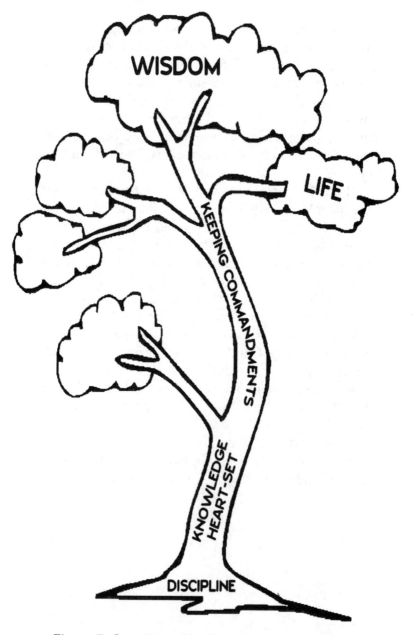

Figure 7. Growth model of the learner's progress

6

Creativity, Level 3

Poet Alfred Houseman wrote that he would walk along thinking of nothing in particular, only looking at things around him and following the progress of the seasons, when suddenly with unaccountable emotion there would flow into his mind a line or two of verse, or sometimes a whole stanza, and a vague notion of the poem which they were destined to form a part of. This story is quoted in books on creativity because it is the "eureka" experience that so many people look for.

The Greek word *eureka* means "I have found [it]." Most of us remember from school days how Archimedes was supposed to have jumped from the bathtub and run shouting "Eureka," because he had just discovered how to apply the principle of specific gravity to the problem of the gold in the king's crown. (Yes, the king had been cheated, the story goes.)

Many others have reported similar experiences. Here

is a psychologist interviewing linguist Noam Chomsky on that topic:

> "Then your discovery of the relationships between your data and the generalizations of your principles is what's really creative for you?"
> "Yes, that's right. That is the creative experience."
> "Are there aesthetic and affective reactions, too?"
> "Yes, that's the whole business! It's the kind of experience I had when I was studying math and logic really seriously and finally got to understand something: the same kind of excitement. Of course I didn't discover it in that case, but in a sense you rediscover it when you finally grasp it, and it's that kind of experience that occasionally comes also from literature or music or something of the sort" (*The Creative Experience*, Ed. Stanley Rosner and Lawrence E. Abt. New York: Dell, 1970, p. 85).

Some report that there is nothing sudden about the creative insight, but there is hard work and passion or getting all steamed up preceding it. Some report heightened perception at such a time. One scientist got his new idea while walking past a row of ugly green houses that he would rather forget, but their particular greenness is forever etched on his mind because of that experience.

Many Christians are familiar with this kind of change in perception, and testify that the world around them took on brighter hues when they were saved or when they came back to God after a backsliding experience. A hymn writer has put it this way:

Heav'n above is softer blue,
Earth around is sweeter green!
Something lives in every hue
Christless eyes have never seen:
Birds with gladder songs o'erflow,
Flow'rs with deeper beauties shine,
Since I know, as now I know,
I am His, and He is mine.
—*Wade Robinson*

The opposite—the dulling effect of being involved with the demonic—is also well-known by novelists and others who write about it.

This illustrates a common theme running through many researches on creativity—that something else is involved besides brain. Aldous Huxley took mescaline to cause a cerebral sugar shortage in order to experience another kind of perception. Some try to trace the creative person's motivation back to his childhood experiences, in the psychoanalytic tradition. Some look to dreams and fantasies, some to the occult.

Could it be that everyone is searching for heart? Is heart the other ingredient needed along with brain to achieve that ultimate, mysterious kind of thinking we call creativity?

The following list of terms is culled from various theories of creativity. Each theory has a contrast between ordinary, logical, conscious thinking and an elusive emotional, unconscious or even supernatural kind of thinking. In most theories the merging of the two is said to be the creative experience. On the left side below are those terms which correspond more closely with what we have been calling head, and on the right side are those with emotional and other aspects more closely associated with heart.

logic	intuition
logic	paleologic
conscious	unconscious
secondary	primary
ego	id
objective	subjective
adult	child
adult	Little Professor
	(an aspect of "child")
left brain	right brain
present life	collective unconscious

"Collective unconscious" is a remarkable phrase that comes from Carl Jung. It is an admission of inability to understand an individual man's thinking to say that he somehow taps a source acquired collectively by mankind. This is similar to tapping the consciousness of the universe, as in a brain theory mentioned in an earlier chapter.

Several well-known theories of creativity focus on phases: preparation, incubation, illumination, and verification. Joseph Wallas first proposed these (*The Art of Thought*. New York: Harcourt Brace, 1926), and they have been imitated with variations by others since then. Later writers point out that this system misses the essence of the creative process. It fails to explain what actually happens at the point of illumination.

J.P. Guilford, in his studies, focused on features of creativity. He came up with the faculty of divergent thinking, which is characterized by flexibility, originality, and fluency. These terms are in the vocabulary of many of us now, and they are what we usually attempt to measure on tests of creativity.

Still a third direction that creativity theories have taken is the Freudian-type search to identify motivations from early childhood. Here is some banter about that from the

74

Rosner and Abt book. The psychologists are interviewing Froelich G. Rainey, archeologist with the enviable accomplishment of finding the long lost city of Sybaris. They are discussing a poem about Sybaris which every European schoolchild was required to learn.

"Do you think that poem by Schiller was responsible for your wanting to find Sybaris?"

"No. Because, as a matter of fact, I never read that poem by Schiller. I can't recall it at all."

"It just knocked our theory to _____!"

"I'm afraid it did. I wish I could support it. Now, it may be that way back in my school days I did read that poem, but I certainly have no conscious memory of it. Sorry about your theory" (op.cit. p. 22).

Some others in the book did identify a motivation dating back to childhood. Enough, I suppose, to keep the theory going. A variation of this is Alfred Adler's "compensatory" theory, that people produce art or science or other creations in order to compensate for their inadequacies or perceived inadequacies.

These theories imply the heart side of thinking. Those theories with phases need motivation to activate the unconscious, or they need primary experience to merge with secondary thinking at the breakthrough point of illumination. The Freudian theory needs motivation in addition to cognition. Only the features-based theories seem to stick mostly to the brain side of thinking. At least this is true of any which use only measurable, cognitive features in thinking. Those who study creative people can come up with heart-type features.

So as we have said, a theme running through most theories is that there is something akin to heart, as well as to brain. Great creative achievements do not come without intense passion on the part of the creator. There often is a vague sort of chaos or disorder and the creative person must make order out of it. It takes both heart and head to do the best job of this.

A commonly used definition of creativity is "bringing order out of chaos." These words naturally make our minds jump to the opening chapter of Genesis, where we read that God brooded over the chaos and then brought order out of it. Now I do not understand what might be included in God's brooding. But I think that many of the scientists and artists I read about in the creativity literature can be said to brood over their problems. Through a combination of working on problems and passionately caring and brooding over them, they may at last bring a new order into their disordered world.

I would like to suggest, also, that there may be a significance to creativity in the fact that God spoke when creating. He said, "Let there be light." Now I am aware of the theological teachings that Jesus is the Word and that He created. There may be many explanations for this fact that God spoke. But I'd like to lay aside for a moment these imponderables and focus on the idea that speaking here implies purposing. God said, "Let there be lights," and the subject content of astronomy was born. He said "Let the earth bring forth grass," and the content of botany was born.

As we saw in Chapter 3, purpose is seated in the heart. Any emotions implied in brooding would also be in the heart. So God's heart was involved, along with His infinite intelligence, in creating an orderly universe. Man, made in God's image, has something of this creative ability. He can make order out of his disorder if he uses both heart and head.

Rollo May wrote a wonderful little book called *Courage to Create* (New York: Norton, 1975). In it he dismisses current theories for two reasons. One is that they are reductive, reducing creativity to some lower process. The other is that they generally make creativity an expression of neurosis. He wrote, "I learned very early in my psychological career to regard with a good deal of skepticism current theories explaining creativity. And I learned always to ask the question: Does the theory deal with creativity itself, or does it deal only with some artifact, some partial, peripheral aspect, of the creative act?" (p. 38).

Then May used several chapters to beautifully present the creative act as encounter. This word may be spoiled for some readers, having been cheapened by its use with psychological "encounter" groups to mean something less than May means by it. Though he does not use the word heart, he seems to be talking about something similar to what I mean when I speak of the merging of heart and head.

Encounter, for May, is complete absorption. There is fusion between conscious and unconscious. There is no longer the split between subject and object. Encounter transcends both, but it is not really outside either. That is, you don't just "let go" with abandon or take alcohol or mescaline to get beyond the confines of your rational self so as to let the artistic, irrational, unconscious self take over. But the total you is fully involved. Emotions and intellect see more clearly together than either can alone.

Western thought is not used to this idea. The dichotomy between subjective and objective, as we have seen, has been with us for four centuries, and one scientist called it the cancer of all psychology and psychiatry. Most systems of psychology assume this split whether or not they are aware of it. We have been taught that we see more accurately if we can be objective and keep our emotions out of it. But May points out that some recent researches show that people see more accurately when their emotions are involved. Reason works better with emotion.

And it may work best of all in that state where subjective and objective are no longer two, but one—in that transcending, "supra" rational state that both May and Maslow have called ecstasy. Here is another troublesome word that means a sort of hysteria in its popular sense. But in its more technical, historical sense it is "ex-stasis": standing out from. Above the split between subject and object, above the split between reason and emotion, is a state some people reach from time to time wherein they see truth more clearly than when they are bound within either way of thinking.

This is not something passive that happens to you. It is something you do, not so much by will power as by commitment to and absorption in a task. May gives the example of a child's play when he is totally absorbed. This is a prototype of adult creativity. The hobby classes and Sunday painting are what May calls "escapist creativity." They are not the real thing because they lack encounter in his high sense of the word.

Stories of how insights, answers, or poems come to people "out of the blue," "in a moment of inspiration," have led some to think that these experiences are happy accidents. But those are only half-stories if they leave out the commitment the person has to solving the problem or writing poems. A full-time writer produced adequately on her job and experienced times of being totally absorbed and inspired. She left her job and intended to continue writing on a part-time basis. Several months later when asked about her writing she answered. "Oh, I haven't been writing anything lately. I write by inspiration and I haven't had any inspiration." A writer uncommitted to anything is not likely to have any "out of the blue" experiences.

What should we do to encourage creativity in our children? The advice to be cautious with discipline because we might stifle children's natural creativity does not fit the biblical theory of this book. Discipline leads to the moral, emotional, and spiritual commitment needed to learn anything creatively or produce anything creative. But this does not mean rigid, conforming classrooms. Many creative people report that formal schooling was stifling. But individual teachers and professors scattered here and there were stimulating.

Our top-notch art teachers may have the right idea. These are the ones who lead children in art and allow them time and freedom for total absorption. Art is an activity in which a good many children can become totally absorbed. In children, this absorption may be one of the main things to aim for. Another is helping them experience secondhand the thrill of creation. Tracing the development of a great science discovery and appreciating great music or poetry lets everyone in on the creative thrill. Still a third approach is to aim as much as possible for an understanding level rather than just the knowing level. As Chomsky said, the thrill of insight for a child is the same as the thrill of a scholar coming upon a new discovery. Through such experiences children learn what new learning is.

The egalitarian view worries about creativity for everyone. A purist view is that only the greats really "have" creativity. And the evolutionary view thinks creativity is necessary if mankind is to pull itself up to a better world.

What should the biblical view be? None of the above. We certainly do not value creativity as a way to save the world. We value it because God put creativity into a person and we value the person. But it is probably not the highest value in education for most Christians. Godliness and character may be highest on our values, and creativity comes somewhere after that. But it merges with other values; people can love creatively and live creatively in many ways.

Among the varieties of creativity is the kind we see in the prophets. When Daniel saw visions in his head, humanly speaking that experience used the subjective more than the objective side of his thinking. Creativity books sometimes cite ancient prophets as examples of the subjective, or of transcendency. But Daniel's source of knowledge was also revelation, which is ignored in the secular writings on knowledge and thinking.

The subjective and objective sides of thinking—or the heart and head—seem to account for differences between scientists and artists. Though all creative activity is a merging of both sides, the final product in some cases falls on the heart side and in others on the head side.

The painter's or the poet's expression is closer to primary, heart experience. But to express subjective "tree" as a painting or poem to be understood by us, requires help from the artist's objective thinking, too. Primary experience and secondary thinking merge in the creative process, and the artistic product falls near the experience end of the spectrum. The scientist, too, may have a creative insight or theory which involved his total person to produce, but the product we see—the new facts about the tree—fall nearer the objective end of the spectrum.

Rosner and Abt interviewed both scientists and artists for their book on the creative experience. These selected people tried to articulate various aspects of the creative experience as they saw it. Reading some of these can enlarge our understanding of ourselves and of possibilities within our children. We notice here some common themes and some disagreements.

Conscious and unconscious thinking:
Froelich G. Rainey, archeologist. It was a rational thing in one way, and it was a kind of emotional challenge in another way.

Wilder Penfield, brain surgeon and writer. Purpose stays with you and a plan. . . . Something becomes plain that was not plain before. That's when the emotion comes in and that's a great thrill. . . . I think it happens as far as I am concerned more when I write and rewrite, and restate the evidence and the information in trying to prepare it for publication. Then very often once I get my thoughts truly expressed I see things I never suspected before.

Arthur Koestler, writer and creativity theorist. One of the real problems in writing, whether it's fiction or non-fiction, is to have one's head in the clouds, but your feet on the earth . . . you are sometimes carried away by a purely abstract flight of thought. . . . Then you bring in an illustration of your abstract idea which pulls you down to reality . . . that bisociation. . . . Hemingway's greatness is that through his monotonously repetitive trivial dialogue, you get glimpses of eternity.

George Nelson, industrial designer. What I think I'm really saying is that you turn off your conscious mind with all its buzzing and scurrying, and just coast. Then the subconscious does the work. We've all heard so many stories: a famous mathematician is worrying about a problem; he goes to sleep and then realizes, when he wakes up, that he has the solution. Well, this is apparently quite a common experience. . . . It is my experience anyway that unless you turn off the active conscious mind, this idea quite possibly won't arrive.

Penfield. And I think that when people say that their brain goes on working during sleep and solves problems, this is probably a false interpretation. The brain doesn't do any working on problems during sleep. But, you come through at the end of sleep with a complete change and with a recollection of the problem and you see it suddenly simplified. Your discovery is there, but it wasn't worked on during the night.

On dreams and fantasies:

Koestler. I mean daydreaming is the opposite of

creativity. Wish-fulfilling fantasies are just the opposite of creative work . . . It would be nice, you know, but it is not the way one writes or creates. It's a burning up of calories to one's own private satisfaction.

Sidney Hook, philosopher. Sometimes striking expressions and phrases come to me in dreams. Occasionally I've used such phrases upon awakening. *(Do you recall ever using the material that has come up in a fantasy or dream?)* No. Only an expression or two.

Seldon Rodman, poet. (Are these prompted by daydreams of yours? By fantasies or nightmares?) No. No. Never.

David Krech, psychologist. There is no question that I do a lot of fantasizing and daydreaming about the research problems that I am working on, and in my fantasies and daydreams, I solve them all. And these solutions, in turn, lead to other and greater achievements! It's a real Walter Mitty routine. But I'm not sure that these fantasies or daydreams provide me with anything more than perhaps motivation or persistence. I doubt that I get any substantive help from them.

Isaac Bashevis Singer, fiction writer. It happens that I dream about something, and, although the dream does not have a direct relation with the topic, still this dream may involve me in an idea. This did happen to me a few times. Another thing is that it might have happened more than I know. Sometimes we forget a dream, but a kind of inspiration is left. We see something in a dream which can later be remembered and become a topic. You never know how much the dream influences reality. [Or how much reality influences the dream. RB.]

Compensatory theory:
Harlow Shapley, astronomer. (Was this idea of showing people something important to you in later life?)

I am afraid that it was important. I suppose it's a matter of vanity. *Morris Kline, mathematician.* I think that in research you want to satisfy your personal ego. You want to know that you did it before the other fellow and then whether he does it or not is no longer relevant. *H. Bentley Glass, geneticist. (Your interest . . . may very well be a real outgrowth of the early influence in your background.)* I'm sure it is. I can't get away from that background. My whole world view is shaped by it.

Rainey. (What was there, if anything, in your family background that predisposed you to an interest in archeology?) I really can't imagine anything, 'cause I was brought up on a cattle ranch in Montana, and my idea of the best life in the world was to be a cowboy. I can't get further away from being an archeologist, as far as I can see.

Koestler. Well, I think an unhappy childhood is a necessary, but not a sufficient, condition for creativity. And mine was a very unhappy one. Like most writers. . . . There was a Russian writer [who wrote], "Everybody has a given amount of calories to burn up—you either burn them up by living or by creating." You can't burn the same calorie both ways. You make poetry out of your unhappiness, and you might argue that you can also make poetry out of your happiness. But why should you make poetry when you are happy instead of living it out? So there must be something unconsummated in the unhappy moments which ask for consummation on a different level.

Rodman. Bach, for example . . . is a man whose problems were resolved almost from the beginning by his complete religious identification with his religion and his particular time and society. In the case of Beethoven, it was much more as it is with the artists today. A constant struggle.

New ideas or solutions from somewhere besides rational thinking:

Ulrich Fransen, architect. (Does accident play a part in your work?) It's absolutely wonderful and I just wish I could design as if my pen had just been slipping all the time. The trouble is that I just get mad at my own rigidity. This is the great thing about the way children draw. It just doesn't have a stylized or a designed look to it. They are just bold accidents. I'm very interested in this and I find the best way to do that is to let my ideas assert themselves though they may not be fully thought out. Ideas just introduce themselves, and I think we're better off for it. I think accident is something really very important.

Shapley. (You actually stumbled upon it?) Well, practically so. After being a kind of intellectual stumblebum, if I may refer to myself in this way, I went after the cepheid variables and, out of much work and with the help of others at the Harvard College Observatory, came the theory of cepheid variation. . . . I think that I initially didn't make much of the implications of this finding. Later on it became clearer that we had had a geocentric universe conception that had been reformulated by Copernicus into a heliocentric one which involved a view of the universe as one in which our sun is central. My new views led finally to a galactocentric conception of the universe in which the central pivot is the galaxy. Using this conception and the implications that seemed to me to flow from it, I had a lot of fun in pouring out one paper after another that sought to develop the material.

Glass. Well, there's nothing sudden about it.

Hook. If a person keeps on writing, he will develop excellent writing ability but, whether he has ideas or not, good or bad ideas, that's something else again. That depends on grace from nature, from God, or elsewhere. Fluency in writing is a matter of habit, but the flash of insight into truth is a gift from somewhere.

Noam Chomsky, linguist. Another approach, which I was following because it intuitively seemed sort of right, though I didn't really believe it [in my head], was working out. I then decided to abandon the first and commit myself entirely to the second. . . . I know that some things get me very excited and other things are just dull. The exciting things are what one wants to follow.

Bonnie Cashin, fashion designer. Ideas just pop into my mind out of the blue seemingly. Sometimes ideas tumble upon each other. Sometimes they just don't come.

An important theme which shows up in the interviews is stimulation by people in other fields with other ways of thinking. A theory of "synectics" has been built around this feature. In this, problems are to be solved by using metaphor and analogy among the diverse fields of the participants in a synectics group.

Numerous other themes are apparent in the studies of creative people, but these already mentioned are enough to show that both heart and head are involved. Even the authors of the book, not writing particularly from a biblical perspective say, "the phenomenological descriptions are enough to start one thinking along mind-body dualistic lines" (p. 383).

That mind part, or the heart and soul of man, is where God communicates with a Christian perhaps more than through body. God the Holy Spirit lives in the heart. He is the teacher. It is not difficult to see that when ideas "come" to man in his most creative moments they come from mind and heart. And a heart controlled by God can create for God's glory.

All creativity needs the other levels of learning to undergird it. Creativity needs good information and concept learning. To those levels we turn now in the next two chapters.

7

Higher Thinking, Level 2

Process is a key word in education writing. It is often opposed to content, as in science classes where students are to learn the ways of science rather than facts of science. They learn how science supposedly attacks problems and arrives at conclusions. Or in history they are supposed to learn the methods of historians. How do historians use primary sources and secondary sources? How do they evaluate and draw conclusions about trends, forces, events, and so forth? It is doing science or history, rather than knowing about science and history.

The reason for doing science is that you might produce science. That is, you might learn new content for others to know. With the new knowledge someone else might do more science and learn something, in turn, for you to know. So the knowing and the doing feed on each other. They cannot be separated.

So there should be no argument about whether process is more important than content, as some make it. We need both. If students do some history of their town or of their school, they learn a few historian skills, and gain some insight about history. And the insight should help them understand history that others have done. But a student could not do his history very well without first knowing quite a lot about other history.

The 1960s and 1970s were a period of great interest in process, but later came a period of renewed interest in content. With some people, knowing (or teaching) content is the whole goal. But others leave a little of process in, while they use content as a vehicle for developing thinking skills. A popular phrase now is "know and be able to do." In writing, for instance, students should know rules and principles, and they should be able to write well.

None of this slicing of human learning or thinking is very neat. Nevertheless, we have to talk about slices and chunks if we were going to talk about it at all. Our Level 2 slice has many elements of process in it. Numerous kinds of understanding are included at this level.

Benjamin Bloom's familiar categories of educational objectives in the cognitive domain show one way to look at the slices. Here, in brief, are his six categories placed into two groups. The first "group" contains only one category, and it might be called Level 1 on the learning model. The second group includes the kinds of understanding that are Level 2 on the model. (*Taxonomy of Educational Objectives.* New York: McKay, 1956).

Knowledge

> 1. *Knowledge:* ability to recall items of information.

Intellectual
Skills
and
Abilities

> 2. *Comprehension:* lowest level of understanding; ability to make use of the material learned.
> 3. *Application:* the ability to use abstractions in particular situations, the

Intellectual
Skills
and
Abilities

abstractions being principles, ideas, theories and such.

4. *Analysis:* ability to break down a learning in such a way that the learning is clarified, organized, and interrelations of the parts shown.

5. *Synthesis:* ability to arrange elements into a pattern or structure which is original, which was not clearly there before.

6. *Evaluation:* ability to judge, compare, and appraise material and methods against a standard or set of criteria.

Level 1 knowledge has a wide range, all the way from "specifics" to "theories and structures." An example of a specific bit of information is that Noah built the ark. An example of a large encompassing structure is a flood theory of geology. Both of these can be known at Level 1. All the other categories—comprehension, application, analysis, synthesis, evaluation—are various ways the mind processes information at Level 2. Synthesis, and others too, can also be Level 3 at times.

At first glance it may seem that complex information has to be Level 2, but a little reflection shows that this is not always so. All we have to do is think of a field of knowledge we know little about. For instance, if we know little physical science, we probably still were told in school about gravity, magnetic poles or electrical charges. But can we use our information? Can we calculate movements, plan experiments, or make predictions with it? If we cannot, we are not even in category 2—comprehension—with our understanding.

If you passed that one, try Beethoven's Ninth Symphony. You may have learned that he wrote it after becoming deaf. You may be able to recall a melody or other details from music appreciation class, but can you analyze its form and harmony, or compare it with other symphonies, or evaluate it in other ways? If you pass this one, you will have to think up your own example. All of us can recall many past learnings in which our understanding is not very high.

Now the big question is, how do we achieve higher level understandings? Or how do we teach so our students achieve a higher level? A good share of education writings revolve around this topic and many suggestions have been given. They may or may not work. The ordinary methods issues are not usually relevant to this question. Though in a specific situation one method at times fits better than others, in a general sense any one method is not the answer to achieving higher level thinking. That is, the methods of TV, lecture, discussion, activity, or others do not determine level of learning. In fact, decades of research on methods has not brought any general consensus about which is best for producing higher level thinking.

If not method, then what? Another place to look is content—the problem of how best to organize content for instruction. A pyramid of content complexity is diagrammed in Figure 8. Facts, at the bottom, are items as close to the actual items or events as possible—the lowest level on the abstraction ladder. In Bible teaching this would be the concrete details of Bible information: Esau hunted wild game, or Esau sold his birthright for a meal of bread and stew.

Above facts, are concepts. They are categories of information: usurper, patriarch, lineage of Christ. A category can be highly inclusive, such as the concept of "history," or it can be such a small category that we have a hard time deciding whether to call it a concept at all or to call it a

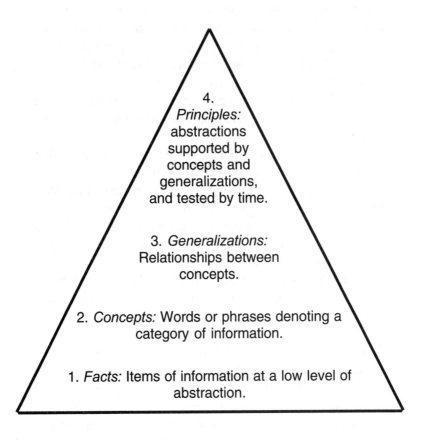

Figure 8. Hierarchy of content complexity

fact. For instance, in the Esau fact examples, the words *hunter, wild game,* and *birthright* have to be learned at some time as concepts—even the word *meal.* But though we can't slice it neatly, our pyramid begins with facts and builds up to concepts. Often the statements are qualified by conditions. An example is: In spite of Jacob's shortcomings, God was working out His plan through him.

At the top of the pyramid is *principles.* These are high levels of abstractions. An example is: God rules in the affairs of men.

Now that we are at the top of the pyramid with a high level abstraction, we may well ask. "What's so hard about that?" It does look simple once we have stated a principle. And we can teach that principle first. We can start either at the top or the bottom of the pyramid. Working from the top down is essentially the deductive approach to learning, and working upward is the inductive approach.

The principle at the top is high level thinking only for those who have the undergirding of the rest of the pyramid. Without that, it is simply fact learning at Level 1. A Sunday school pupil, for instance, may hear his teacher say that God rules in the affairs of men. And he may remember it. But does he understand how Jacob fits into that principle? Further, at school studying history, government, or economics, can he apply the principle in his thinking? Does it make a difference in his beliefs or his understanding of events and theories? If he has processed it to the high level of a principle, it will, but otherwise it remains a Level 1 fact.

A good way to make learning dull is to constantly treat abstractions as Level 1 learning. Children, particularly, lack a rich background of experience and understandings, and a history book full of abstractions holds little meaning for them. In arithmetic, the numerals and the way we handle them in computation are the abstractions, and children must understand the concrete meaning behind these if they are to learn arithmetic at Level 2 rather than Level 1.

Sometimes the back-to-basics movements ignore this need to build understandings. In their desire to get on with the solid stuff they just teach everything as facts. Principles, generalizations, conclusions, and so forth are simply facts to be learned and tested and scored. Some students may reach higher level thinking anyway. But not all.

For example, I offered a friend a newsletter from a mission organization I am interested in. "I would like to introduce you and your husband to this organization," I said as I held out the letter. She backed off and would not touch the letter. It looked as if I were offering poison. She explained that she had learned in college which mission organizations were "good." This one, I said, was new since her college days; she might want to see what it was doing. But no, she would abide by the Level 1 learning of twenty years earlier. She would not read, evaluate, judge or do any higher thinking about the matter. She had no way to add anything to her approved list, and she also had no way to drop an organization if it should change character over the years. Her higher level thinking was not developed.

To encourage the higher thinking at Level 2, we can work up the pyramid or down, and, in fact, work up and down intermittently, moving upward to see relationships, moving down to find a concrete example, back up to think about conclusions, and so forth.

One way to plan a learning sequence is to begin by giving a generalization at the top. This provides a framework. It tells students where their subsequent learning is going to lead, what they are going to understand, or what rule they will be able to use. Students with higher intelligence profit more from this approach.

The opposite way to plan a learning sequence is to start at the bottom with numerous concrete facts. When a student understands these, build up to concepts and generalizations about the facts. Or in some cases build up to a principle. If students can formulate or discover a generalization for themselves, so much the better. But in classroom teaching there comes a time when the teacher should explain so that all can have a chance to understand, including those who were not able to work things out for themselves.

For a good illustration of these matters of inductive, deductive, and discovery learning, we can look at the great reading debate, which seems to be perennial. The debate was fiery in the 1960s and that brought to those times a resurgence of phonics and a new approach called linguistic. Together these were classed as "decoding." The word *linguistic* has since fallen into disuse, although the contributions of the linguists have permanently changed the way phonics is organized and presented to children. And the debate continues to flare up.

During the height of the debate, I was teaching in Alaska. A prominent senator and his entourage made a three-day (!) tour of Alaska and became expert on Alaskan reading problems. "I saw a train on a village school bulletin board," the newspaper quoted him as saying. "No wonder the children couldn't read," he continued. "They need books about dog sleds and snow machines."

In our teachers' lounge a first grade teacher said, "I have never seen a subway. I wonder how I learned to read about them." The rest of us added palaces, dragons, jungles and other topics we loved to read about as children. How did we ever learn from stories such as those?

Well, the senator got a large appropriation for the development of Alaskan reading books and, presumably, a boost for his presidential hopes. But reading problems live on.

I have taught hundreds of people, all ages, at the beginning stages of reading, and I think the content of their first books is not important at all. At that early stage, the mind is occupied with the excitement of figuring out the words and discovering patterns. That thrill can suffice for a time without worrying about how the story will turn out.

Now, I do believe that children need books in their homes, stories read to them, and all those things. And a boy turned off to reading might be turned on again by a book about his favorite football player. All that is true. But it is not the heart of the beginning reading problem.

Can you remember learning to drive? Especially with manual shifting? You concentrated on pushing the clutch in, not the brake, pulling the lever to exactly the right position, steering all the time, eyes on the road, checking the rear view, and so on. Intense concentration. You didn't say, "This is too dull; I want better scenery. I should have dogsleds around me instead of Dick and Jane and Father."

This is the sense in which I say that the content of first books hardly matters. The mechanics of reading are enough to occupy the mind. That is, it occupies the mind if reading is taught from a system that believes in mind.

The behaviorist system does not believe in mind. Just show the word (stimulus) and reward the right response. With enough repetition and rewarding, the words will be learned. Critics call this the look-say method. It is Level 1, and if used exclusively or for too long it lacks mental challenge.

Phonics systems vary in the thinking levels they use. Some systems start with learning most of the sounds and their spellings, and rules for using them. Then children are supposed to reason deductively at Level 2, and start figuring out words and reading. My opinion is that young children using this system do not do as much of this deductive reasoning as their teachers assume. A second grader looks at *treat*. First he has to see the two vowels and decide to use his rule, "When two vowels go walking, the first does the talking." Then he has to remember other rules about that vowel *e* and its long sound, as well as his learnings about the consonant sounds. If he remembers all the rules and can apply them, he reads *treat*. (This happens not to be an exception to the rules.) Brighter children may actually do all this, but many children cannot do so much deductive reasoning at so young an age, even if they do manage to memorize all the facts this system requires. Some children get by, anyway, because of so much repetition in the teaching. And many, I'm sure, actually use inductive thinking that other phonics programs use.

The phonics systems that are arranged for inductive thinking owe much to the linguists who refined the order in which to present language information to beginning readers. These systems usually begin with short *a,* but sometimes with another vowel. Then with only a few consonant sounds added, the beginners learn to read words in the consonant-vowel-consonant pattern, such as *pat* and *tap*. As children learn more sounds, they fit them into the pattern and they gain an idea of how reading will proceed. As they continue with this system, children discover patterns for themselves, and at some point they don't need the rest of the phonics their teachers had planned for them. This higher thinking is more stimulating than memorizing sounds and rules at Level 1 thinking. Those sounds get memorized, anyway, as children use them and incorporate them into patterns they formulate.

Because of their one-on-one teaching, homeschooling parents who happen to buy reading texts arranged this way catch on immediately to the value of this system. These days they call them "phonics readers" instead of "linguistic readers."

As the child grasps the marvelous patterns in the language and forms them into generalizations of his own, his excitement is as great as Noam Chomsky's when he was formulating profound new generalizations about language. What does it matter that the content is the "Nan had a fan" type in the early stages of this system?

Now this inductive reasoning is not a panacea to take all the problems out of reading. But lacking neurological problems or other hindrances, it can be a remarkably fast route to reading. I have seen first graders with slightly above average intelligence learn to read quite well in the first five weeks of school. Other children can learn that fast if we wait until they are a little older to teach them. I have seen adult non-readers learn to read with only sixteen hours of instruction. This is the power of Level 2 insight learning.

Inductive learning is not necessarily superior to deductive. Both kinds of thinking are needed. Scientists and artists operate sometimes one way and sometimes the other. This dichotomy can also be expressed as whole versus part. In studying a piece of literature you may want to enjoy the whole, to get an overall view, and then begin analyzing parts, to relate them to the whole, seeing how the writer accomplished his effects, and other purposes you may have for studying it.

Along with arranging content for higher thinking, we must also work within the developmental level of the pupils. The letter *e* and the sounds of *e* are concrete, and it's around age 6 to 7 that children on the average become able to reason with concrete items. Children who cannot do this reasoning have trouble with reading approaches that require reasoning. The books on teaching your baby to read, you will notice, rely on repetition and association—Level 1 learning.

At age 11 to 12 children begin moving into abstract reasoning. Here we can give them lots of help and practice. The concepts and abstractions they can reason with are necessarily quite simple for a long time. Political and social ideas, for instance, are often far too complex. They take more background of experience and knowledge than children this age have. A survey once showed that seventh graders have little understanding of taxation, and showed also that a good many seventh grade teachers skipped that topic if it was in their books. They had learned from experience that the children couldn't get it.

The following transcriptions from sixth grade classes show one way that teachers can encourage higher level thinking at ages where children are not very experienced with it yet. The abstractions here are mostly character traits. Children know about these from real life and from stories. So they have a better chance to "think" than if the topics were taxation, inflation, or international relations.

In the first example, notice the discussion never gets off the ground. The the children are not practiced enough to relate, generalize, or apply, and the teacher lacks a specific plan to help them. To the final application question the children give pat answers apparently at Level 1. As you read the transcription, picture a class with, usually, several hands raised. So when the teacher calls a name she is simply acknowledging one whose hand is raised. She is not arbitrarily calling on child after child as it may appear on paper. The class has just read the Bible story of Esther, and now we listen in.

Teacher: What did the story mean to you, Debbie?
Debbie: Umm, I can't think.
Teacher: Tom?
Tom: Well, it was exciting.
Teacher: Exciting. What did it mean to some of the rest of you? Greta?
Greta: The way Queen Esther helped her people.
Teacher: Anything else? Mandy, what did you think the story meant? *(No answer.)* Eric?

Eric: Well, just about Queen Esther. No, not just about Queen Esther but about Haman and Queen Esther.

Bob: And Mordecai.

Teacher: Bob thinks Mordecai is important too. Debbie, do you remember now?

Debbie: Yes. That you shouldn't hate people.

Teacher: Why do you say that, Debbie? Will you explain why you thought it meant that?

Debbie: Well, Haman, he hated the Jews.

Teacher: All right. Cindy?

Cindy: Well at the end, what the story meant to me was Haman, well he wanted to kill the Jews so he was killed himself.

Teacher: Tom, you wanted to say something.

Tom: Well, see, like Mordecai, well he just helped the king to save his life, and Queen Esther wasn't afraid to go, and the king could order anything. That's all.

Teacher: Greg?

Greg: When Queen Esther went to the king's big, uh, throne room he loved her and he held out his scepter.

Jon: And she didn't have to die.

Teacher: Jon, what did you say?

Jon: She didn't have to die.

Teacher: Yes. Lisa?

Lisa: Well, in every Bible story there's a lesson, and in this story there's a lesson too. That you shouldn't do bad things.

Teacher: So you think the story has a lesson to teach us. Any other thoughts about the meaning of the story? Debbie?

Debbie: You shouldn't want to do bad things to people.

Teacher: Roger?

Roger: You should love people.
Teacher: Any other ideas? Ralph? *(No answer.)* Did you all like the story?
Students: Yes.
Teacher: Why did you like it?
Students: Because it was good.

In another class, the teacher worked out a questioning sequence that began at the bottom of the pyramid and worked upward, as on Figure 9. Her first question simply drew out facts and reviewed the story. She asked, "What happened in this story?" In an adult class you would probably skip this repetition of the story. The next two planned questions were intended to help build concepts of the characters of Haman and Mordecai, using the facts just reviewed. She asked, "What happened that told you what kind of man Haman (or Mordecai) was?"

After the children worked at these awhile she sprang a question that would let the children use the two concepts they had just been talking about. She asked, "What differences do you see between Mordecai and Haman?" They had the job of contrasting the two men. This is a kind of relating—the third slice up the pyramid.

The teacher's culminating question was, "Do you think this story has a meaning for us?" The men's characters were different, and concrete things that happened to them in the story were different. One man came to a happy ending, and one to a sad ending. The children draw on these concrete happenings, as well as on the characters of the men, in trying to give answers. Insofar as they succeed, they have found a principle—the top slice of the pyramid. If something applies to Haman and Mordecai, and also to people in our times, then it can be called a principle.

Watch the upward progress of this class. It is larger than the other and, again, many hands are waving. The

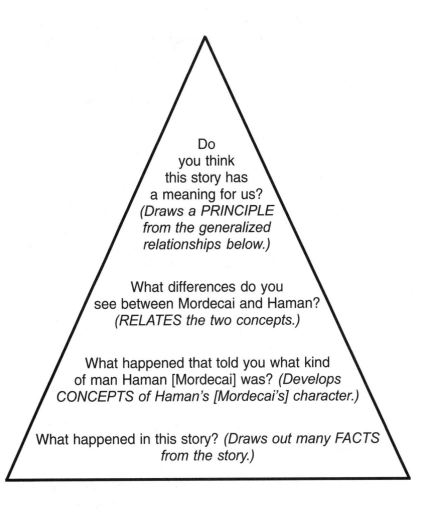

Do
you think
this story has
a meaning for us?
*(Draws a PRINCIPLE
from the generalized
relationships below.)*

What differences do you
see between Mordecai and Haman?
(RELATES the two concepts.)

What happened that told you what kind
of man Haman [Mordecai] was? *(Develops
CONCEPTS of Haman's [Mordecai's] character.)*

What happened in this story? *(Draws out many FACTS
from the story.)*

Figure 9. Questioning Pyramid for Story of Esther

teacher calls individuals by name so as to keep only one talking at a time. The key questions are labeled for you.

Teacher: What happened in this story? Fred?
(facts)
Fred: Well, a lot of things, It's about Queen Esther saving her people.
Ivan: And Mordecai.
Teacher: Mordecai? What about Mordecai?
Ivan: He helped too. Helped save the people.
Teacher: And what else happened? *(The discussion continues a few moments on the first question. We take it up again further along.)*
Hugh: Boy, Haman was really a mean man.
Teacher: You think he was mean. Let's talk about Haman
(concept 1) for a while. What happened that told you what kind of man Haman was? Matt?
Matt: Well, you could tell what kind of guy he was. He wanted to kill all the Jews.
Teacher: Any other ideas? Peggy?
Peggy: He hated the Jews.
Teacher: Anything else in the story that told you about Haman? Ivan?
Ivan: He wanted everyone to bow to him.
Teacher: Hugh, what were you going to say?
Hugh: The same thing.
Teacher: Okay. Who can think of something else? Wendy?
Wendy: Oh, I remember something. It might not be what you want. It's a little thing, maybe, not important, but he bragged to his family and said how great he was.
Teacher: He bragged. That's important. Now let's think
(concept 2) about Mordecai. What happened that told you what kind of man he was? Fred?
Fred: Well, he worked in the king's palace.

Teacher: Kristi?
Kristi: He put on sackcloth and cried for all the Jews.
Teacher: Ivan?
Ivan: He cried and stuff, but he did a lot of other things for the Jews. He told Esther she should go to the king and if she didn't go she would get killed anyway so it's all right if the king might kill her.
Teacher: Wendy?
Wendy: The king loved her so he wouldn't kill her.
Teacher: Yes. Is there anything else that told you about Mordecai? Hugh?
Hugh: Well, he kinda, well, you know, he was like a leader and sent letters and things to all the Jews.
Teacher: Kristi? I see you have something to say.
Kristi: Yeah. He took Esther, sort of like adopted her, and he didn't have to do that, and so, and he did it anyway, and it tells us what he was like.
Teacher: Yes. Now what would you say are differences
(relation-ship) between Haman and Mordecai? Matt?

Matt: Well, for one thing Haman wasn't, he wasn't a Jew and Mordecai and Esther were Jews.
Teacher: Haman wasn't a Jew and Mordecai was. Give us some other ideas. Peggy, you have one?
Peggy: Yes, that's why he hated them. And Mordecai didn't hate people. That was different.
Teacher: One of them hated and one didn't. Wendy?
Wendy: Well, I think, well, Mordecai helped the king. Like it said in the books, he saved the king's life.
Natalie: I think you could say Haman helped the king too. He was, what you call it, like second ruler in the kingdom. That's helping.
Teacher: So you think they both helped the king. Do you see any differences in the way they helped? Wendy?

Wendy: Yes. Maybe it's not, but I think Mordecai was, well, he was loyal to the king.

Natalie: Maybe Haman was loyal too. How do you know he wasn't?

Teacher: Aaron? You want to answer that?

Aaron: I think the king would rather have Mordecai working for him. He could trust him. He wouldn't do anything bad.

Teacher: You think the king could trust Mordecai more than Haman. What was different about Haman?

Aaron: Well I . . .

Teacher: Kristi?

Kristi: Haman was just interested in being great himself. He probably wouldn't think about the king so much.

Teacher: All right. So this story told you a lot of things *(applica-* about Haman and Mordecai. Do you think this *tion)* story has a meaning for us? Hugh?

Hugh: Well, not to be like Haman.

Teacher: Aaron?

Aaron: It does a good job of showing about a good man and a bad man, and in the end it came out, well, both of them got what they deserved.

Teacher: Matt?

Matt: Well, yes it has a meaning, and I think it shows how people can be mean to you sometimes but God works it out in the ending.

Teacher: Fred, you wanted to say something?

Fred: Well, I think it has a meaning because it was kinda like a miracle. Esther was made queen just in time, like Mordecai said, just so she could save the people.

Joe: God made it happen.

Teacher: You say God made it happen. What are you really saying about the meaning of the story for us?

Joe: I'm saying, uh, well, God could do it for us too. I mean if we were in trouble and everything.

Teacher: All right. Peggy?

Peggy: I think it does a good job of showing how some people don't realize about quite a few things.

Teacher: Now can you be more specific? What don't they realize about?

Peggy: Oh, things like God and . . . they don't realize that they shouldn't hate and . . . I mean, I know you don't get saved by being good, but, but . . .

Teacher: But you think we should be good anyway?

Peggy: Yes.

Teacher: All right. Joe?

Joe: They don't realize that they can't just get great by themselves. I mean, God makes it. Haman was bragging that he did it.

Children who have done their own thinking in this way have more to remember. The higher level processing gives them a Level 2 insight and not just Level 1 knowledge. The hope is, also, that the thinking skills they gain will transfer to other situations.

In summary, we have shown that the content of phonics and other curriculum can be organized in ways that encourage a higher level of thinking. The curriculum itself does not always do this. Minds are bigger than our theories, and many students will see patterns and relationships no matter how poorly the curriculum may be organized. But our efforts in this direction will help many more children to achieve this kind of thinking.

In this chapter we have focused mainly on Level 2 of cognitive learning, the left side of the model. Now we move to memory, which is both Level 1 and also Level 2, as we have seen here, since higher level insight learning is a powerful aid to memory.

8

Memory, Levels 1 and 2

Tom Sawyer was getting ready for Sunday school one morning, and part of the routine was his memory work. He had chosen five verses from the Sermon on the Mount "because he could find no verses that were shorter." Patient cousin Mary was helping.

"Blessed are the—a—a—"

"Poor—"

"Yes—poor; blessed are the poor—a—a—"

"In spirit—"

"In spirit; blessed are the poor in spirit, for they—they—"

"Theirs—"

"For theirs. Bless are the poor in spirit, for theirs is the kingdom of heaven. Blessed are they that mourn, for they—they—"

"Sh—"

"For they—a—"

"S, H, A—"

"For they S, Sh—oh, I don't know what it is!?

"Shall!"

"Oh, shall! for they shall—for they shall—a—a—shall mourn—a—a—blessed are they that shall—they that—a—a—they that shall mourn, for they shall—a—shall what? Why don't you tell me, Mary? What do you want to be so mean for?"

The story doesn't tell whether Tom remembered these particular verses long enough to earn his tickets, but he had his own system for collecting tickets. He traded "likrish" and fishhooks and other valuables for them, and he eventually accumulated enough to be awarded a Bible. When a distinguished visitor was present, Tom chose that day to claim his prize. This led to great embarrassment for the superintendent but much hilarity for the readers.

That was Mark Twain's way of poking fun at the system of memorizing used in his day. He perhaps gave no thought to memory theory, but if he had he would have said he was writing about the "mind is a muscle" theory. By that old theory, the more you exercise your mind the stronger it gets. Tom's Sunday school teachers were trying to motivate the children to exercise their memories.

Since Tom's day there has been a staggering amount of research and writing on memory, more than on creativity. No one person could read and organize all the research reports. Books have been written presenting various organizations of the research, and now they are so numerous that even organizing the organizers is too large a problem for one chapter to handle.

But that is not necessarily a loss to us. The amount of research is no indication of the amount of knowledge, and over and over in the literature you will read about how little we know of memory. Piling up the researches or stringing them end to end does not add up to a complete view of how memory works.

When you reflect upon your own mind and what you can do with it, you have a pretty good idea about a lot that research doesn't know. Scientific research only lets objectively gained information into its system. Though that is something, it is by far the smaller part of mind.

In this chapter we look at that smaller part for some of the insights it can give us. First, in relating memory to the three-level learning model, we have to include both lower levels. Memory is more than what people mean when they speak of rote learning in a deprecating way.

Rote implies learning without understanding or thought. To put it in the computer terms so often used today, we would say that between input and output there is no processing or manipulating, no relating to past learning, no transforming or elaboration. But there is output, a repeating of the input. The word memorizing often has this connotation, and it refers to word-for-word repetition of poems, multiplication tables, and so on. Since we are not computers with mindless wires arranging the output, there is a little understanding, a little processing of some kind, even in the lowest level of learning. And the amount of processing can vary to as high as Level 2 on the learning model.

As far back as the 1920s, psychologist Charles Spearman wrote of two levels of mental action—one that recognizes and reproduces, and the other which leads to new mental content. Arthur Jensen, a later memory researcher, wrote of two levels in memory. He used the terms in essentially the same meaning as on our learning model. Level II was characterized by more complexity and not by more difficulty. For example, on intelligence tests you are sometimes asked to repeat lists of numbers. The longer a list is, the more difficult it is to repeat. But the thinking on such lists is on Level I.

Level 2 functioning is dependent on Level 1 ability, both in Jensen's memory research and in the broader aspects of the learning model in this book. But the reverse is not true. People can be adept at Level 1 memorizing, while not understanding at Level 2. This happens at times with certain kinds of mental retardates. As intelligence rises, Level 2 functioning rises with it, so that this level might be equated with what has been called a "general intelligence."

I find it useful to divide the theories into two groups: 1) those which see memory as one of the "faculties" of mind, and 2) those which see memory in a wholistic context related to a complex mind. These categories may be diagrammed as in Figure 10. But for our two levels of memory we need to cut across the columns as in Figure 11.

Tom Sawyer memorized quite definitely at Level 1, just repeating word for word without bothering to understand. He also aimed for short-term memory. He wanted to remember the verses only long enough to say them when he arrived at Sunday school. After that he could forget them.

An important theme in memory research is that of short- and long-term memory. Short-term memory has a limited holding capacity of about seven items, plus or minus two. On average, adults can repeat at least five digits immediately after hearing them. By chunking digits together we can increase memory span to more digits, but the total chunks of information remain within the limits which average about seven. Chunking means to read 2714 as "twenty-seven, fourteen" instead of "two, seven, one, four." That's two chunks instead of four. A phone prefix of 185 should be read as "one eighty-five." We hear this as either one chunk or two chunks depending on whether we mentally visualize it as a one-hundred number. Thus a phone number is reduced to three or four chunks instead of the memory limit of seven. If hearing it on the radio, we usually must add 1-800. If radio announcers would learn how to

Faculty theories	Organization theories
Studies require simplification and measurement in the tradition of Ebbinghaus of the nineteenth century. His book, *Memory*, was translated into English in 1913.	Studies assume a wholeness of the human mind, a richness and complexity not measurable. This approach was used by F. C. Bartlett in *Remembering*, 1932.

Figure 10. Memory Theories

	Faculty theories	Organization theories
Level 2 Learning		Relating new learning to old, adapting existing mental schema to incorporate new information, organizing, manipulating, and processing in various ways to make it possible to store information and to call it up from storage.
Level 1 Learning		Learning by association, repetition, practice, perception, so as to put out essentially what was put in.

Figure 11. Memory Levels

chunk these numbers they could get by with repeating a phone number only twice instead of three times, which seems to be the irritating standard now. We do not need formal research to prove this to ourselves. We only need to try it on a couple of people to see that if we chunk the numbers they can hold it in short term memory long enough to copy the number without having three repetitions.

Besides chunking, research shows us other techniques to use. One is to distribute the practice. Tom would have done better to spend a few minutes on his verses at several points throughout the week instead of doing it all on Sunday morning. He could have gotten by with less total time.

Another technique is concentration. Memory researchers often write of "mental rehearsal." Mary could have said to Tom, "Now I'll say a line and count to ten. Then you say the line back to me." With this tricky little procedure, Tom would have spent ten seconds rehearsing the line to himself. Mary should count silently, so as not to interfere with his thinking.

The physiological reason this works is that it takes time for the memory trace to be made in the brain. As energy flows through the nervous system with new information, it makes changes in the cells. In the first few seconds a sort of holding pattern can be formed in the brain and a person will be able to retrieve information from that pattern for several hours. Consolidation of the pattern happens after several hours if conditions are right, particularly if there is no interference or blockage. It is most important that interference not come within the first few seconds. That is when many items are lost from short-term memory, and they never get to long-term storage at all.

Of course we do not want to remember everything that bombards our senses. We are selective. But for those items we select to learn, we need to allow time. I notice this when I look up an item in a book index. There may be two pages I want to check, and if I turn immediately to the first page and read a paragraph there, then I forget what the other page number is and I need to refer to the index again. But if I take a few seconds to learn both page numbers, I remember them long enough to look up both pages.

So time is required for new learning. It also is required for review. Some Scripture memory programs use various schedules of diminishing reviews, reviewing often at first and then less and less often. This is exactly the right thing to do, according to researches.

All the techniques mentioned so far more or less ignore meaning—the techniques of distributed practice, repetition, rehearsal, and spaced reviews. That is because these come from research which tries to isolate a memory function from the rest of thinking, in the Hermann Ebbinghaus tradition as shown in Figure 10. F.C. Bartlett objected to Ebbinghaus' approach as being too artificial. In real life people do not learn nonsense syllables by repetition and without associated meaning. Yet this was what researchers were measuring and scoring.

Bartlett contended that a human "effort after meaning" was important. He suggested that we have "schemata" (plural) in our minds from past learning, and we try to fit new learning into the existing schemata. To show this, he used stories told rather unclearly and involving bizarre happenings, such as with ghosts. When people retold the stories after hearing them, they made changes which showed their own understandings of the events.

Bartlett's book is considered a classic in early memory research, but it did not start a tradition as did Ebbinghaus' work. His theory was too vague and complex to be tested by the kind of research in vogue.

Piaget, in his work with children, demonstrated the effect of mental schemata upon memory. In one of his tests he used a board arranged as in Figure 12. We look at the grid and see two kinds of order or series. We see cards arranged by size in rows, with the largest in the top row and each following row successively smaller. Then in the columns, we see them arranged by color, from dark to light.

With this schemata in our minds, with this understanding of the double seriation—both size and color—we would have no trouble remembering the pattern and reproducing it from memory. But children who are too young to understand seriation cannot produce a copy from memory. Those a bit older, who understand single seriation, may get the sizes right but the colors scrambled.

In other words, understanding has a lot to do with memory. It is not just a stimulus-response operation. The stimulus of seeing the pattern is not enough. We have to first process the information—taking notice of the decreasing sizes and diminishing colors and lumping that information into patterns in our minds. People "code" such information in various ways. Two common ways of coding are imagery (figural) and semantic (verbal). Some of us do better at processing images and others do better at processing semantic meaning.

Imagery as a memory system has been taught from the time of the Greeks, down through Dale Carnegie, and more recently, Jerry Lucas. These imagery systems are forms of association learning, in which you associate an image with an item you want to remember. This is one of the simplest, or lowest, forms of learning. That is to say that association is a simple kind of meaning; there is not a high level of meaningful relationships to understand, but only the meaning of association, and sometimes even these meanings are contrived.

For instance, Carnegie taught people to memorize *run* for *one*, *zoo* for *two*, *tree* for *three*, and so forth. After memorizing the basic "pegs" a person can learn a list of other items by association with these. The first item on the list is associated with run in some sort of mental image, the second with zoo, and the third with tree, and so forth. If you are memorizing your grocery list you try to make a mental image of bread running, catsup behind bars in a zoo, and lettuce sitting in a tree. Then you just look through your images of run, zoo, and tree, and recall the other item in each image. It is sometimes said that sillier images are better than more ordinary ones, but research has not borne this out.

Some people easily produce vivid mental images, and they do exceedingly well with these imagery memory

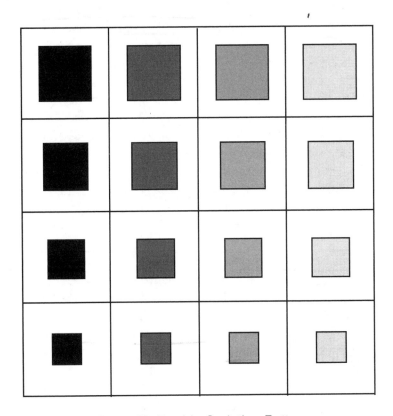

Figure 12. Double Seriation Pattern

systems. They amaze us verbal people with their mental gymnastics and the prodigious amounts of memorizing they accomplish by this means.

At times we might wish we could improve our memories so that we could remember just everything. But we should be grateful that we cannot. Our thinking depends on being selective about what we perceive, what we make images of, and what we store away in our memories.

A famous example of imagery gone wild was documented by the Russian psychologist, A.R. Luria (*The Mind of a Mnemonist*. New York: Basic Books, 1968). Luria's subject (S) saw so many images that they crowded in upon him, interfering with his thinking. Where most of us try to learn how to remember, S tried to learn how to forget. Everything turned to images in his mind. Even speech sounds emerged as lines, blurs and splashes. Sounds had form, color and taste. One time S asked an ice cream vendor what flavor she had. The tone of her answer, "Fruit ice cream," conjured up an image of coals and black cinders coming out of her mouth so that S was unable to buy any ice cream from her. S said that other people think while they read, but he saw while he read. And the images piled up until they became positively distracting to any thinking. If an image provoked a thought, then that thought brought a new image to replace the one he started to think about, and in this way he got led far afield. He could not even recognize people's faces because he made such good images of every expression that he was confused by the constantly changing moods and expressions on faces.

This is image-making in the extreme. One of our great strengths in thinking is that we can ignore most stimuli around us. We abstract only certain features about a person's face and from these few features recognize it as the same face a moment later or days later. In a sentence we abstract a certain thought or thoughts and dwell on those in our thinking. An image or feel or taste of every phrase, word or letter sound does not intrude when we do not want it to. We code only certain information as images.

Some of us prefer semantic coding and use it more than image coding. In memory research, one technique is to show a series of pictures to subjects, and ask them to make up a sentence about each picture. This adds semantic meaning to the mere seeing or to whatever imaging the memorizers may do, and this helps them remember the pictures better.

This technique is an easy way to improve memory. Just talk to yourself about something you want to remember. Say something about it. This forces you to process it mentally. You evaluate it in some way, form an opinion, compare with past learning, or observe more closely to note details. In one or more of these ways you expand the meaning of an item by the simple procedure of saying something about it. This gives you more associations to remember it by, a more complex neural pattern in the brain and more routes by which it can be retrieved from memory.

When you are introduced to someone you can just look at the face and say. "How do you do?" But if you want to add semantic meaning, you can say to yourself that she looks a little like Aunt Ellie, although probably younger. With that extra meaning, you are more likely to remember the person if you see her again.

Some items we want to remember need to be condensed rather than expanded. In preparing for a history test or trying to remember a sermon, people condense into outlines or other kinds of notes. They memorize the framework and hope to reconstruct the other details as needed. Most people tend to code semantically in numerous ways. It does not have to be as formal as an outline to count as semantic coding.

Coding by imagery and semantic meaning are not the

whole of our memory. For example, we might see other reasonings surrounding the coded items we retrieve from memory. We can decide whether an item is accurate, whether it is appropriate to the present problem and other such evaluations. Our thinking, then, even in the simple part we call memory, is always more than the reductions described by research. But research can give us a few hints about a better way to memorize.

For memorizing literary material, such as Scripture passages, the whole method is superior to the part method in three ways. It results in:

1) more efficiency
2) more meaning
3) longer retention.

Tom Sawyer was using the part method, and his parts were as small as one or two words. From such small parts he got very little meaning. He did not relate the words to each other and that's why he could not remember what came next.

The same principle applies with larger parts and a longer whole. If you learn one verse at a time until they add up to a whole chapter, you will spend a lot of your memorizing time trying to learn which verse follows which. But if you work on the whole chapter at once, the interrelations of the parts, the organization, and other aspects will be more meaningful.

The first step in memorizing a whole chapter is to read through it with concentration. If you have never tried this system, you might read through a chapter and then think, "This is a stupid idea. How am I ever going to learn this all at once?" Well, it's not really all at once, and you're on your way. You are now more familiar with it than before you read it. Read it some more. Or listen to it if you prefer. After a few days, try saying the parts you know and reading the parts you don't know while going straight through the whole chapter. By now you are on step 2 of this 4-step plan.

1. Become familiar with the whole unit.
2. Practice the whole unit many times with concentration.
3. Work extra on difficult parts, if necessary.
4. Overlearn.

It takes a little ingenuity to keep yourself motivated and concentrating. You can use a tape in your car, have someone listen and prompt you, or simply read the parts you need prompting on. Manage this latter system by slowly sliding a paper or card down the chapter as you recite, uncovering after you say the words when you can, but when necessary uncovering before you say the words.

People who try the whole method find it really works. It takes less time. And when they are finished they can recite smoothly through a chapter without worrying about which verse comes next.

While the largest part of memorizing may be the motivation, only a small percentage of the research has been on motivation—less than five percent according to Michael Eysenck, one of the compilers of memory research. One chapter of Eysenck's book, *Human Memory*, evaluates research on "arousal." Arousal is measured by physiological changes such as skin conductance or pupil contraction in the eye. Results of this kind of research are equivocal. It is complicated by various factors of whether they are measuring arousal at input or output, whether they refer to short-term or long-term, and what type of memory task it uses.

But arousal does have effects of various kinds. One generalization is that high arousal reduces the number of cues that are taken in. The question of inner mental tasks versus receiving outer information, as in the Laceys' research (chapter 3), is not considered in these researches. Perhaps that would straighten out some of the problems.

So over 95 percent of the research looks into behaviorist matters such as how many nonsense syllables you remember fifteen minutes after learning them, one day later, and one week later. And the remaining small percentage looks into motivation. In some of these, people are motivated by wanting to avoid the electric shock they will receive if they miss. The more general kind of motivation that we all know affects our learning and remembering is not touched.

I remember when I was a child, probably about ten, I was in competition with one of my sisters to make the highest number of points on memory at Vacation Bible School. Each afternoon I practiced on the front porch with a brother or sister as listener. A younger sister listened in on the sessions to hear what I was learning, then she learned the same verses. And each morning her points totaled as much as mine. Or if I learned something secretly and got ahead, she found out from the memory secretary and managed to catch up the next day. My only hope was to learn something on the last day just before the books closed. And it had to be long enough that she couldn't do it quickly, too.

So I chose the Ten Commandments—Exodus 20:3-17. At recess I hid in a pew, read the verses over with the highest concentration I ever had in my life, and then repeated them to the memory secretary. And that was not simply short-term memory, as for years afterward I could repeat those verses more easily and with greater accuracy than most other passages I had learned.

Teenagers, with the motivation of quizzing on teams, memorize whole chapters and books of the Bible. Probably most people who have done any amount of memorizing could tell about something they memorized more easily or more quickly because of high motivation.

Periods of heightened motivation may not come often and probably should not be the norm for learning. But a heart for learning and the discipline to undergird it are necessary for all learning. A professor at Yale recently said that universities have money, equipment, facilities, and techniques as never before, but they are losing their soul.

Christian education has not yet lost its soul. In schools where a Christian atmosphere still reigns there is purpose for learning and desire to learn. There is good motivation and the needed discipline for getting on with the job of learning. To this heart side of learning we turn once again for the closing chapter.

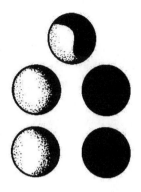

9

The Heart Side

In Christian education writings, a prominent topic has been how to talk to children about their personal salvation. We were told to avoid phrases like, "Come into my heart." Instead, we were to say, "Come into my life" or some other phrasing that does not use the word *heart*. A lot of energy went into thinking up alternative wordings to use while teaching children, in order to avoid treating the heart as something real.

The dominant teaching about heart in these writings was that the word was merely a figure of speech for the seat of our emotions, and we must not confuse children, who would think of a physical blood pump. Children could do a lot with hearts on Valentine's day and at other times, and it didn't seem to me that they were confused. When I was a child, I dressed two chickens every Saturday and I don't think it confused me; I could cook a chicken's heart and draw a Valentine heart without mixing up the two.

The only Christian I met who did worry about the

physical blood pump was an Eskimo man who questioned a childhood song about the color of the heart. His teachers taught, "My heart was black with sin until the Savior came in." This man's testimony said that he knew a seal's heart was red; so why did the song say hearts were black and then white?" At least that's not Scripture; it's a song. Isaiah says that though "our *sins* be as scarlet, they shall be as white as snow" (1:18), but the Bible does not say anything about the color of our hearts.

Also, the Bible does not give a hint anywhere that its use of the word *heart* is figurative and not literal. Since *heart* is used almost 1000 times without such a hint, that sends a strong message that the Bible is talking about something real and literal. So all the discussion about how to avoid the word *heart* when talking to children was wasted effort.

It is not only the Bible that uses the word *heart* in ways presented in this book, but more medical people these days are researching this difficult problem of heart. The Laceys (chapter 3) have done further research since the first edition of this book. Paul Pearsall, a heart transplant physician, in *The Heart's Code* (1998, Broadway Books), reports on several other researchers, including himself. This topic does not lend itself well to what we might call "hard science," because everything we want to measure is quite subjective. It is difficult to get numbers that look like science. Pearsall wrote, "Until we can find other ways to measure 'L' energy (his term for 'life energy')—we must use a brain-oriented means to try to access our heart's code and to interpret the behavioral signs in our body that reflect the nature of the energy of and from our heart" (p. 29).

Pearsall adds life energy to the physicists' four energies—gravity, electromagnetism, and strong and weak nuclear energy. Life energy makes a fifth. Could he be reaching for the God energy that Paul wrote about when he said (of Jesus) that "by him all things consist" (Colossians 1:17)?

A hundred years ago most scientists still believed in a life force in living things which made them different from non-living things. But now as a result of science, most scientists, non-Christian at least, have a mechanical view of the human body and greet the heart research with skepticism.

An event in my own family removed my last skepticism. My grown son Andy was in intensive care after a bicycle accident. His total brain was injured, one side under pressure from a large blood clot inside the skull and the other side all bruised. He could talk but did not say anything coherent. The nurses would start counting or reciting the alphabet trying to get Andy to count to ten or to say part of the alphabet. At an early stage of recovery he could not do this. I decided to try Scripture passages that I knew Andy had memorized, so I began, "In the beginning was the Word..." and Andy could continue from there, reciting several verses of the chapter. So it seemed that the heart knowledge resided somewhere besides the brain, or maybe in addition to the brain.

Pearsall uses terms like "heart memory" or "cell memory." Some of his patients, he wrote, were more heart sensitive than others. A most dramatic story was told by a psychiatrist at a professional meeting. Her patient was an eight-year-old little girl who was the recipient of the heart of a murdered ten-year-old girl. The recipient screamed at night with recurring nightmares about a particular man. The psychiatrist and the mother decided to call the police, and with the child's descriptions and information, the police found the murderer (*op.cit.* p. 7). Some of Pearsall's patients with new hearts gained a craving for Mexican food, or used new words in their vocabulary, or in other ways picked up information that could be traced to their heart donor.

Physicists want more than anecdotes to form their

theory of a "fifth force," but this is difficult to study because it exists not in one place but everywhere all the time. Here is one experiment designed by the United States Army Intelligence and Security Command. Some white blood cells were scraped from a volunteer's mouth. They were centrifuged, placed in a test tube, and an emotion detector (lie detector) inserted, too. In a separate room the volunteer watched a TV program with violent scenes. Even though the mouth cells were in a separate room, a polygraph detected extreme excitation in the cells when scenes of fighting and violence were shown. This experiment was repeated a number of times, with the cells being separated up to fifty miles and up to two days after donation of the cells (*op.cit.* p. 43). Pearsall observed that it is possible that what we now call paranormal may soon be called normal.

Dr. Randolph Byrd, in San Francisco, conducted prayer experiments with patients undergoing heart surgery. Prayer groups scattered around the world prayed for some of the patients, and those patients did significantly better than the ones who were not prayed for.

These are not rare or isolated events. In 1979 at Princeton, a program was set up called Princeton Engineering Anomalies Research (PEAR). For more than twenty years they conducted more than a million trials to study the interaction of human consciousness, not with other humans, but with machines. In small but measurable amounts they found that humans can affect whether the machine will become less random in putting out ones and zeros, and other results that only engineers can devise.

Many teachers and parents know intuitively about teaching to the heart. This is probably a major reason that homeschoolers do so well. In academic tests, the homeschool children on average score well above the national average, and it doesn't matter whether their parents are trained teachers, college graduates, high school graduates only, or anything in between. Some schoolteachers-turned-homeschoolers say they have to unlearn most of what they learned about teaching. Homeschooling is largely heart to heart. The methods and even the curriculum do not matter nearly as much as the relationship between child and parent.

Many Sunday school teachers, too, have always tried to reach their students heart to heart. In the mid 1900s, churches were being inundated with published curriculum, teacher training meetings, and much learning about fashionable teaching methods. One teacher, typical of many, said, "It doesn't seem right anymore. I used to plan how I could get the Scripture into the hearts of my students, but now I find myself thinking about the methods I'm told to use and I'm not even thinking about the Scripture."

On the heart side of our model (page 48), the right lower level begins with discipline. In this important matter, we are not likely to get the best guidance from secular science. Discipline and love go together. They are inseparable in the Bible. Without love, an adult may control, repress, or keep a child in line, but he cannot truly discipline. He cannot help the child grow his inner discipline, and build his life and learning toward more mature levels. Discipline needs love, and love requires that we discipline. Only the heart knows how to wed these together.

Some humanist systems in discipline, such as Teacher (Parent) Effectiveness Training, try to combine discipline and love. They don't always use the word love. They may speak of caring, involvement, or warm relationships instead. Behavior modification, theoretically, takes none of this into account, operating on the basis of rewards. But the main reason that works as well as it does, is that someone cares enough about a child to try the system with him.

Glasser's reality therapy applied to schools is sort of

a positive thinking approach of helping children learn to control themselves. Glasser did not use the word *punishment,* but spoke of reasonable consequences of behavior. This could go by the name of Responsibility Therapy, since children are given more freedom and responsibility as they show themselves able to handle it. Reality therapy has some good, workable ideas, and I think this system is closer to biblical principles than any other secular system. Glasser said love and worth are two basic needs. When children feel loved and worthwhile there are no discipline problems. Minor altercations, perhaps, but not the kind of trouble that comes consistently from a child who carries it with him.

Now if love is so important a part of discipline, we Christians ought to be better at it than the non-Christian world. We should be leading the way, both in theory and in practice. And a good theoretical system should have a blending of love and discipline.

Though the pendulum at times swings back from permissiveness to discipline, practically everyone in psychology is reluctant to go as far as advocating corporal punishment. Political movements, which hold the behaviorist view also, work to eliminate corporal punishment. Yet many Christians insist on their rights to use it since the Bible advocates it. We are all dichotomized as being "for" or "against."

Seeing the issue as black or white in this way is not likely to secure either political solutions or research insights. We need to change the question to "when" corporal punishment is useful. And that answer will be tied to the heart attitude of the child rather than to particular actions.

Verses supporting corporal punishment are found in the Bible. Correcting and chastening can take various forms, but here are some verses where they definitely mean physical hurt. "He that spareth his rod hateth his son: but he that loveth him chasteneth him betimes....Foolishness is bound in the heart of a child; but the rod of correction shall drive it far from him....Withhold not correction from the child: for if thou beatest him with the rod, he shall not die. Thou shalt beat him with the rod, and shalt deliver his soul from hell" (Proverbs 13:24; 22:15; 23:13,14). Even these strongest of verses show that one should use punishment with love and with concern for the child uppermost.

In a Christian school one day a little boy's orange fell from his desk and rolled up the aisle. A fellow second grader picked it up and walked back to return it. The boy who got out of his seat was made to stay after school and receive a spanking. The rule was to stay in your seat, and he had broken it. This dictatorial approach is insensitive to the child as a person. It sets up rigid authority and absolute submissiveness as major values, and uses corporal punishment to enforce them. There is no consideration about what might be in the child's heart. Did he have foolishness in his heart that needed to be driven out by the rod? Was he rebellious in his general attitude? Was he rebellious even against this one rule? Or did he in kindness of heart simply forget for a moment about the rule? The heart question is major in such situations. With this approach we no longer have a yes or no question about corporal punishment. But we have questions of when and how and in what kinds of situations.

In the Bible, the word for punish also means to chasten or discipline or instruct. The two ideas of punish and teach are inseparable. This is the Hebrew word *yacar*. A former generation mother might have said, "I'll learn you" as she approached with her rod for spanking. She had the word exactly right.

Control by power works well enough for Level 1 discipline and Level 1 learning. That is, if the schooling is the non-thinking type, if it consists of rote learning of spelling words, multiplication tables and such, then the power approach to discipline can work. If all you want is Level 1 behavior, you can get it this way. As one psychiatrist put it, a man will even dig his own grave if you point a gun at him. But if the schooling is to achieve any inner discipline, or higher thinking, a higher method than brute force must be used.

To move on to higher levels, beyond the early discipline, we can explore the tasks in the spiritual developmental lists given below. This chart is arranged so that each earlier task on the list is necessary for the later tasks. We have seen, for instance, that a child must experience discipline in his early years in order to develop self-discipline in later years. And this discipline is a prerequisite for the other kinds of learning on the list. A good attitude toward self in the early years is necessary for a growing awareness of and concern for others in later years.

This characteristic of sequence holds even when children do not have the normally good home and church environment that the list assumes. If a child comes to school "retarded" in spiritual development because he did not experience love or learn of God in his preschool years, that is where you have to start with him. Some "remedial" work is needed before you move on to the higher level tasks.

So one characteristic of this list is that the tasks have a logical, positive relationship across the ages. That is, the earlier tasks lead to the later. Earlier tasks are readiness for the later. Earlier tasks cannot be skipped to arrive at the later ones.

A second characteristic of the list is the logical inter-relationships of tasks at any one age. For instance, at the preschool level those who hear about God and Jesus in an atmosphere of love, security, and joyfulness are the ones likely to be developing good attitudes toward them. And those who experience love and discipline are those who can develop concepts of right and wrong. At an elementary level, those who are gaining the important basic Bible teachings will be increasingly aware of the need for Christian love and responsibility in their relationships with others. Put another way, if development in one area is poor for a child, his development in the other areas is likely to be poor also. And good development in one area helps along with it good development in the others. They grow together.

So these spiritual tasks can be seen as: 1) being interrelated at each age level; and 2) being sequentially related across the ages. This listing makes for what might be called an expanded definition of Christian growth. This definition breaks it down into smaller pieces. With smaller pieces, we can better analyze where children are and can be more specific in our goal setting.

Spiritual Developmental Tasks of Preschool
1. Experiencing love, security, discipline, joy and worship.
2. Beginning to develop awareness and concepts of God, Jesus, and other basic Christian realities.
3. Developing attitudes toward God, Jesus, church, self, Bible.
4. Beginning to develop concepts of right and wrong.

Spiritual Developmental Tasks of Elementary School Years
1. Receiving and acknowledging Jesus Christ as Savior and Lord.
2. Growing awareness of Christian love and responsibility in relationships with others.
3. Continuing to build concepts of basic Christian realities.
4. Learning basic Bible teachings adequate for personal faith and everyday Christian living, including teachings in these areas:
   a. prayer in daily life

b. the Bible in daily life

c. Christian friendships

d. group worship

e. responsibility for serving God

f. basic knowledge of God, Jesus, Holy Spirit, creation, angelic beings, Heaven, Hell, sin, salvation, Bible literature and history.

5. Developing healthy attitudes toward self.

Spiritual Developmental Tasks of Adolescence

1. Learning to show Christian love in everyday life.
2. Continuing to develop healthy attitudes toward self.
3. Developing Bible knowledge and intellectual skills adequate for meeting intellectual assaults on faith.
4. Achieving strength of Christian character adequate for meeting anti-Christian social pressures.
5. Accepting responsibility for Christian service in accordance with growing abilities.
6. Learning to make life decisions on the basis of eternal Christian values.
7. Increasing self-discipline to "seek those things which are above."

Spiritual Developmental Tasks of Maturity

1. Accepting responsibility for one's own continued growth and learning.
2. Accepting biblical responsibilities toward God and toward others.
3. Living a unified, purposeful life centered upon God.

When goals are listed as above, it is an attempt to use our heads to try to understand spiritual and heart matters. Sometimes we have to do this; Pearsall wrestled with the same problem in his book, *The Heart's Code.*

Today we can easily see the failures of trying to teach heart matters to the head and not the heart. Whether teaching about drugs or unplanned pregnancy or whatever, when the schools took up the topics the problems only got worse. Homeschoolers do a great job of teaching those difficult topics because much of their teaching just naturally is heart to heart. Learning about methods and curriculum is not the route to that kind of teaching.

For many Christian workers it is difficult to change their way of thinking to a more literal interpretation of the word *heart*. After years of assuming that they could say heart but really mean mind or brain, that system of thinking is difficult to discard. One man, after hearing about the Bible view of heart, said, "Yes, some cultures say heart and other cultures may say liver (Lamentations 2:11) or something else." This statement seems to mean that different words in different cultures are figurative ways to speak of the mind, when actually they are old ways of speaking that have come down to us correctly. The Bible uses liver or bowels or inward parts as it uses heart for the seat of emotions (Genesis 43:30, I Kings 3:26, Isaiah 6:11) and our common speech retains some of those usages, such as when we say we have a "gut" feeling.

Paul Pearsall also uses terms besides the heart for the usual mind functions to reside. He speaks of "cell memories" in various parts of the body. Pearsall himself had a bone marrow transplant, and because of having someone else's cells within him, he felt that he had much in common with heart transplant patients. He joined them in the hospital halls as they talked in their informal support groups.

We cannot go wrong by using the Bible terminology. We can talk to children about having Jesus in their hearts and they will understand. We can speak of broken hearts, heavy hearts, gut feelings, and other such terms that reside in our language. The old ways are more true than some of the new "scientific" research would tell us.

Appendix A
Research Data on *Heart* in the Bible

This research on Bible uses of *heart* was done at Tennessee Temple Seminary by Kenneth Clark and Jack Noble. It is now the most complete research of this Bible word to be found anywhere. In Hebrew, this is the word *leb* or *lebab*, and in Greek *kardia*. The King James translators occasionally translated the Hebrew word as *mind*, and these uses are included here, since it is the same original word.

The total number of uses of *heart* in the Bible is found here to be 981. Other writers on this topic have come up with slightly different totals, probably because of the differences in working strictly from English translations or from the original languages. But in any case, the total is almost 1000 occurrences. Other writers, some with only a cursory attention to counting, always come to the conclusion that the main meanings of *heart* have to do with soul, mind and inner being, rather than with the physical blood pump. The physical is the most seldom used meaning in the Bible, amounting to only 1.6% in this research.

Researcher Kenneth Clark states it this way: "Mankind is not, as the behaviorists would have you believe, just another animal nor as the humanists propose just another type of biochemical machine that can be enhanced or developed into a better human machine. But rather, mankind was created in the image of God with an eternal immaterial heart . . ."

The first six categories used here came originally from chapter 3 of the first edition of this book. In order to validate their work of categorizing, these researchers compared their results with references in Brown, Drivers, and Brigg's *Hebrew and English Lexicon of the Old Testament*, and with Thayer's *Greek English Lexicon of the New Testament*, as well as with the illustrations given in chapter 3 of this book. They found a validation of 88% of agreement with these sources. This is a very high figure, especially considering that often two or more categories are meant and the problem comes down to deciding which is dominant. These researchers added a category of "combination," which more accurately reflects some uses of the word *heart*. They also added a category called "general," which speaks in a holistic way of God's heart, of a person's heart, or even of a lion's heart. Words included in the combination or general categories are counted only once and not counted also in other categories.

The highest category of all is that related to thought, mind, or our cognitive functions. Nearly one-fourth, or 24.8%, of the total is found here. The next highest is the moral uses—21.7%. These have to do with good or evil, or turning to or from God. The third highest category is emotion—17.9%. These have to do with love and hate, joy and sorrow, and so forth. There is no indication in Scripture that these uses of *heart* are figurative; they are as literal as any of the other categories. The remaining three major categories are spiritual (14.3%), motivation (6.9%), and physical (1.6%).

On the following pages are the totals and percentages for each category, shown for each major section of the Bible as well as for the grand totals, and then the data of this research, listing every occurrence of the word *heart* and its reference. In the proper column after each reference is inserted one or more words to try to describe briefly the meaning intended for that occurrence of *heart*. Often these words come directly from the Bible, but sometimes in the interest of brevity another wording is used.

SUMMARY: FIGURES AND PERCENTAGES

	Thought	Motive	Spiritual	Moral	Emotion	Physical	Combination	General	Totals
Pentateuch	32 26.7%	13 10.8%	18 15.0%	9 7.5%	25 20.8%	4 3.3%	16 13.3%	3 2.5%	120
History	28 14.4%	25 12.8%	37 19%	30 15.4%	41 21.0%	5 2.6%	23 11.8%	6 3.1%	195
Poetry/Wisdom	84 29.4%	10 3.5%	28 9.8%	72 25.2%	55 19.2%	5 1.8%	29 10.1%	3 1.0%	286
Prophecy	49 23.3%	11 5.2%	20 9.5%	58 27.6%	40 19.0%	1 .5%	25 12.0%	6 2.9%	210
Old Testament Totals	193 23.8%	59 7.3%	103 12.7%	169 20.8%	161 19.9%	15 1.8%	93 11.5%	18 2.2%	811
Gospels	21 32.8%	2 3.1%	8 12.5%	20 31.2%	6 9.4%	1 1.6%	5 7.8%	1 1.6%	64

SUMMARY: FIGURES AND PERCENTAGES

	Thought	Motive	Spiritual	Moral	Emotion	Physical	Combination	General	Totals
Acts	6 25.0%	1 4.2%	7 29.2%	3 12.5%	5 20.8%	0 0%	2 8.3%	0 0%	24
Pauline Epistles	16 24.6%	5 7.7%	20 30.8%	15 23.1%	4 6.2%	0 0%	5 7.7%	0 0%	65
General Epistles	6 42.9%	0 0%	1 7.1%	6 42.9%	0 0%	0 0%	0 0%	1 7.1%	14
Revelation	1 33.3%	1 33.3%	1 33.3%	0 0%	0 0%	0 0%	0 0%	0 0%	3
New Testament Totals	50 29.4%	9 5.3%	37 21.8%	44 25.9%	15 8.8%	1 .6%	12 7.1%	2 1.2%	170
Grand Totals	243 24.8%	68 6.9%	140 14.3%	213 21.7%	176 17.9%	16 1.6%	105 10.7%	20 2.0%	981

(Note: percentages are rounded to the nearest tenth)

BIBLE REFERENCE DATA

	Thought	Motive	Spiritual	Moral	Emotion	Physical	Combination	General
Ge 6:5	thoughts							
Ge 6:6			grieved the Lord					
Ge 8:21a			Lord said				imagine evil	
Ge 8:21b	*			*				
Ge 17:17	said							
Ge 18:5						bread for heart		
Ge 20:5				integrity				
Ge 20:6	speaking			integrity				
Ge 24:45	said							
Ge 27:41								
Ge 42:28					failed			
Ge 45:26					fainted			
Ex 4:14				*	glad			
Ex 4:21			*	*			Lord hardened	
Ex 7:3		set	*	*			Lord hardened	
Ex 7:13			*	*	was hardened		Lord hardened	
Ex 7:14			*	*			Lord hardened	
Ex 7:22					he hardened			
Ex 7:23					was hardened			
Ex 8:15					he hardened			
Ex 8:19					was hardened			
Ex 8:32								
Ex 9:7			*	*				
Ex 9:12							Lord hardened	
Ex 9:14								plagues upon heart
Ex 9:34					he hardened			
Ex 9:35					was hardened			
Ex 10:1a			*	*			Lord hardened	
Ex 10:1b			*	*			Lord hardened	

	Thought	Motive	Spiritual	Moral	Emotion	Physical	Combination	General
Ex 10:20			*	*			Lord hardened	
Ex 10:27			*	*			Lord hardened	
Ex 11:10			*	*			Lord hardened	
Ex 14:4			*	*			Lord hardened	
Ex 14:5		turn against people						
Ex 14:8			*	*			Lord hardened	
Ex 14:17			*	*			God will harden	
Ex 15:8								midst of sea
Ex 23:9	know							
Ex 25:2		willingly						
Ex 28:3	wise							
Ex 28:29						heart organ		
Ex 28:30a						heart organ		
Ex 28:30b						heart organ		
Ex 31:6a			Lord put wisdom					
Ex 31:6b	wise							
Ex 35:5		willing						
Ex 35:10	wise	stirred						
Ex 35:21		willing						
Ex 35:22	wise							
Ex 35:25		stirred						
Ex 35:26		willing						
Ex 35:29		may teach						
Ex 35:34								
Ex 35:35	wisdom		Lord put wisdom					
Ex 36:1	wise							
Ex 36:2a	wise							
Ex 36:2b								
Ex 36:2c		stirred						

	Thought	Motive	Spiritual	Moral	Emotion	Physical	Combination	General
Ex 36:8	wise							
Le 19:17				hate				
Le 26:16					sorrow			
Le 26:36					faintness			
Le 26:41				uncircumcised				
Nu 15:39		seek						
Nu 16:28	mind							
Nu 24:13	mind							
Nu 32:7					discourage			
Nu 32:9					discouraged			
De 1:28					discouraged			
De 2:30			Lord made heart obstinate					
De 4:9	not forget							
De 4:29		seek						
De 4:39	consider							
De 5:29			Lord said					
De 6:5			love Lord					
De 6:6	words							
De 7:17	say							
De 8:2	to know							
De 8:5	consider							
De 8:14				lifted up				
De 8:17	say							
De 9:4	speak							
De 9:5				uprightness				
De 10:12			serve the Lord					
De 10:16				circumcise				
De 11:13			serve the Lord					
De 11:16	deceived							

	Thought	Motive	Spiritual	Moral	Emotion	Physical	Combination	General
De 11:18	lay up words		love the Lord					
De 13:3								
De 15:7	*				not harden			
De 15:9				*			thought/wicked	
De 15:10					grieved			
De 17:17			turn not from God					
De 17:20					not lifted up			
De 18:21	say				hot heart			
De 19:6					fear not			
De 20:3								
De 20:8a					faint hearted			
De 20:8b		set			faint hearted			
De 24:15			keep command-ments					
De 26:16			Lord will smite					
De 28:28								
De 28:47					joy/gladness			
De 28:65					trembling			
De 28:67					fear			
De 29:4	perceive							
De 29:18	saying		away from Lord					
De 29:19a	imagine							
De 29:19b	call to mind							
De 30:1			obey Lord					
De 30:2								
De 30:6a				circumcise				
De 30:6b				circumcise				
De 30:6c								
De 30:10			turn to Lord					
De 30:14	word							all heart

	Thought	Motive	Spiritual	Moral	Emotion	Physical	Combination	General
De 30:17	not hear						set mind to words	
De 32:46	*	*						
Jos 2:11					melt, fear			
Jos 5:1					melted			
Jos 7:5					fearful			
Jos 11:20			*	*			Lord harden	
Jos 14:7	word in heart							
Jos 14:8					melt			
Jos 22:5			serve God					
Jos 23:14	know							
Jos 24:23			incline to Lord					
Jg 5:9		toward						
Jg 5:15	thoughts	searching of heart						
Jg 5:16		follow						
Jg 9:3								
Jg 16:15	not told							
Jg 16:17	told							
Jg 16:18a	told							
Jg 16:18b	shewed							
Jg 16:25					merry			
Jg 18:20					glad			
Jg 19:5						comfort, strengthen		
Jg 19:6					merry			
Jg 19:8						comfort, strengthen		
Jg 19:9					merry			
Jg 19:22					merry			
Ru 3:7					merry			

	Thought	Motive	Spiritual	Moral	Emotion	Physical	Combination	General
1 Sa 1:8					grieved			
1 Sa 1:13	spake							
1 Sa 2:1					rejoiceth			
1 Sa 2:33					grieve			
1 Sa 2:35			God's heart					
1 Sa 4:13					trembled			
1 Sa 6:6a					you harden			
1 Sa 6:6b					they hardened			
1 Sa 7:3a			unto Lord					
1 Sa 7:3b			unto Lord					
1 Sa 9:19	tell							
1 Sa 9:20	mind							
1 Sa 10:9			God gave					
1 Sa 10:26			God touched					
1 Sa 12:20			serve Lord					
1 Sa 12:24			serve Him					
1 Sa 13:14			Lord sought	*				
1 Sa 14:7a		*					do according to heart	
1 Sa 14:7b								thy heart
1 Sa 16:7			Lord looketh					
1 Sa 17:28				naughtiness				
1 Sa 17:32					fail, fear			
1 Sa 21:12	words							
1 Sa 24:5	*			*	*		heart smote him	
1 Sa 25:31					no offence			
1 Sa 25:36					merry			
1 Sa 25:37						died		
1 Sa 27:1	said							
1 Sa 28:5					trembled			

144

	Thought	Motive	Spiritual	Moral	Emotion	Physical	Combination	General
2 Sa 3:21					desire			
2 Sa 6:16					despised			
2 Sa 7:3		go do						
2 Sa 7:21			God's heart					
2 Sa 7:27	*		*				Lord pray	
2 Sa 13:28	think				merry			
2 Sa 13:33		toward						
2 Sa14:1								
2 Sa 15:6		*		*	*		stole heart	
2 Sa 15:13		*		*	*		heart after Absolom	
2 Sa 17:10a					melt			
2 Sa 17:10b								heart of lion
2 Sa 18:14						thrust through		
2 Sa 19:14a					bowed			
2 Sa 19:14b					bowed			
2 Sa 19:19	remember							
2 Sa 24:10				*	smote himself			
1 Ki 2:4	*	*	*		*		all their heart	
1 Ki 2:44				wickedness				
1 Ki 3:6				uprightness				
1 Ki 3:9	understanding							
1 Ki 3:12	*							
1 Ki 4:29	*							
1 Ki 8:17		in heart to build						
1 Ki 8:18a		in heart to build						
1 Ki 8:18b		in heart to build						
1 Ki 8:23		*	*	*			all their heart	
1 Ki 8:38	*				plague of heart			
1 Ki 8:39a								God knows heart

	Thought	Motive	Spiritual	Moral	Emotion	Physical	Combination	General
1 Ki 8:39b	*							God knows heart
1 Ki 8:48	*	*	*	*	*		all their heart	
1 Ki 8:58			incline to God					
1 Ki 8:61				perfect				
1 Ki 8:66					glad			
1 Ki 9:3			Lord's heart					
1 Ki 9:4				integrity				
1 Ki 10:2	communed							
1 Ki 10:24	*	*	*				God put wisdom	
1 Ki 11:2								
1 Ki 11:3			away from God					
1 Ki 11:4a			away from God	not perfect				
1 Ki 11:4b			away from God	perfect				
1 Ki 11:4c								
1 Ki 11:9			turn from God					
1 Ki 12:26	said		turn to Lord					
1 Ki 12:27	devised							
1 Ki 12:33	*	*	*	*	*		all heart	
1 Ki 14:8								
1 Ki 15:3a				not perfect				
1 Ki 15:3b				perfect				
1 Ki 15:14				perfect				
1 Ki 18:37			turned to God					
1 Ki 21:7					merry			
2 Ki 5:26	heart went with							
2 Ki 6:11					troubled			
2 Ki 9:24						arrow at heart		
2 Ki 10:15			Lord's heart	right				
2 Ki 10:30								
2 Ki 10:31			not in law of Lord					

Reference	Thought	Motive	Spiritual	Moral	Emotion	Physical	Combination	General
2 Ki 12:4		give from heart						
2 Ki 14:10				proud				
2 Ki 20:3				perfect				
2 Ki 21:7					merry			
2 Ki 22:19					tender, tearful			
2 Ki 23:3			walk after Lord					
2 Ki 23:25			turn to Lord					
1 Ch 12:17		be knit						
1 Ch 12:33				double heart				
1 Ch 12:38a				perfect				
1 Ch 12:38b				all of one heart				
1 Ch 15:29					despised			
1 Ch 16:10					rejoice			
1 Ch 17:2	*	*	*	*			do all in heart	
1 Ch 17:19			Lord's heart					
1 Ch 22:7		minded to build						
1 Ch 22:19		*	*				set to seek Lord	
1 Ch 22:25		in heart to build	heart to pray					
1 Ch 28:2				perfect				
1 Ch 28:9				perfect				
1 Ch 29:9			God tries heart					
1 Ch 29:17a								
1 Ch 29:17b				uprightness				
1 Ch 29:18a	thoughts							
1 Ch 29:18b		*	*				heart to God	
1 Ch 29:19	asked			perfect				
2 Ch 1:11								
2 Ch 6:7		in heart to build						
2 Ch 6:8a		in heart to build						
2 Ch 6:8b		in heart to build						

	Thought	Motive	Spiritual	Moral	Emotion	Physical	Combination	General
2 Ch 6:14			walk with God					God knows heart
2 Ch 6:30a								God knows heart
2 Ch 6:30b								
2 Ch 6:38			return to Lord					
2 Ch 7:10					merry			
2 Ch 7:11		in heart to make						
2 Ch 7:16			Lord's heart					
2 Ch 9:1	communed							
2 Ch 9:23	*	*	*				God put wisdom set to seek Lord	
2 Ch 11:16		*	*				not set to seek	
2 Ch 12:14		*	*					
2 Ch 13:7		*	*		tender		set to seek Lord	
2 Ch 15:12								
2 Ch 15:15	sworn			perfect				
2 Ch 15:17				perfect				
2 Ch 16:9			ways of Lord					
2 Ch 17:6		*	*					
2 Ch 19:3							set to seek Lord	
2 Ch 19:9			heart not to God	perfect				
2 Ch 20:33			*					
2 Ch 22:9		*					sought Lord	
2 Ch 24:4		minded to repair						
2 Ch 25:2				not perfect				
2 Ch 25:19				lifted up				
2 Ch 26:16				lifted up				
2 Ch 29:10			covenent with Lord					
2 Ch 29:31		willing		upright				
2 Ch 29:34		heart to do						
2 Ch 30:12								

	Thought	Motive	Spiritual	Moral	Emotion	Physical	Combination	General
2 Ch 30:19		*	*				prepared to seek God	
2 Ch 31:21			serve in God's house					
2 Ch 32:25				lifted up pride				
2 Ch 32:26								
2 Ch 32:31	know							
2 Ch 34:27				tender				
2 Ch 34:31			keep commandments					
2 Ch 36:13			*	*	he hardened			
Ezr 6:22							God turned heart	
Ezr 7:10		prepared						
Ezr 7:13		minded to go						
Ezr 7:27			God put in heart					
Ne 2:2					sorrow			
Ne 2:12		heart to do					God put in heart to do	
Ne 4:6		mind to work						
Ne 6:8	heart feigns							
Ne 7:5		*	*					
Ne 9:8			faithful					
Es 1:10					merry			
Es 5:9					glad			
Es 6:6	thought							
Es 7:5		presume						
Job 1:5			curse God					
Job 7:17		set						
Job 8:10	utter words							
Job 9:4	wise							

	Thought	Motive	Spiritual	Moral	Emotion	Physical	Combination	General
Job 10:13		*	God's heart	*				
Job 11:13			*				prepare	
Job 12:24			God takes away heart					
Job 15:12	understanding			away from God				
Job 17:4	thoughts							
Job 17:11	lay up words							
Job 22:22								
Job 23:16			God makes heart soft					
Job 27:6				reproach				
Job 29:13	heart followed	*			*		caused joy	
Job 31:7	eyes							
Job 31:9				deceived				
Job 31:27	enticed							
Job 33:3		set		uprightness				
Job 34:14				hypocrites				
Job 36:13								
Job 37:1					trembles			
Job 37:24	wise							
Job 38:36	understanding							
Job 41:24					leviathan's heart hard			
Ps 4:4	commune							
Ps 4:7					gladness			
Ps 7:9			God trieth	upright				
Ps 7:10				*				
Ps 9:1		*	praise with heart					
Ps 10:3							wicked desire	

	Thought	Motive	Spiritual	Moral	Emotion	Physical	Combination	General
Ps 10:6	*						said, not moved	
Ps 10:11	said							
Ps 10:13	said	*						
Ps 10:17			God prepared					
Ps 11:2				upright				
Ps 12:2	*			*			spead with double heart	
Ps 13:2					sorrow			
Ps 13:5					rejoice			
Ps 14:1	said							
Ps 15:2	*			*			speaks truth	
Ps 16:9					glad			
Ps 17:3			God proves heart					
Ps 19:8					rejoicing			
Ps 19:14	meditation							
Ps 20:4		desire of heart						
Ps 21:2			God gave					
Ps 22:14					melted			
Ps 22:26			Lord's heart					
Ps 24:4				pure				
Ps 25:17					troubles			
Ps 26:2			Lord try heart					
Ps 27:3					fear			
Ps 27:8	said							
Ps 27:14			Lord strengthen					
Ps 28:3				mischief				
Ps 28:7a			trusted Lord					
Ps 28:7b					rejoiceth			
Ps 31:12	from mind							
Ps 31:24			Lord strengthen					

	Thought	Motive	Spiritual	Moral	Emotion	Physical	Combination	General
Ps 32:11				upright				
Ps 33:11			Lord's heart					
Ps 33:15			Lord makes heart					
Ps 33:21					rejoice			
Ps 34:18					broken			
Ps 35:25	say							
Ps 36:1	saith							
Ps 36:10								
Ps 37:4			Lord's heart	upright				
Ps 37:15				sword enter heart				
Ps 37:31				law in heart				
Ps 38:8					disquiet			
Ps 38:10						panteth		
Ps 39:3					hot			
Ps 40:8				law in heart				
Ps 40:10				righteousness				
Ps 40:12				heart faileth				
Ps 41:6				integrity				
Ps 44:18				turn back				
Ps 44:21	*		*				secrets God knows	
Ps 45:1	inditing							
Ps 45:5								heart of enemies
Ps 49:3	meditation							
Ps 51:10				clean				
Ps 51:17				broken				
Ps 53:1	said							
Ps 55:4					pained			
Ps 55:21				war in heart				
Ps 57:7				fixed aright				
Ps 58:2		*		*			work wickedness	

	Thought	Motive	Spiritual	Moral	Emotion	Physical	Combination	General
Ps 61:2					overwhelmed pour out			
Ps 61:8		set						
Ps 61:10		*						
Ps 64:6				*			search iniquities	
Ps 64:10								
Ps 66:18	*			upright			regard integrity	
Ps 69:20			Godly heart		broken			
Ps 69:32				*				
Ps 73:1				clean				
Ps 73:7	wish							
Ps 73:13				cleansed				
Ps 73:21					grieved			
Ps 73:26a						flesh & heart faileth		
Ps 73:26b			God is strength					
Ps 74:8	said							
Ps 76:5				stout heart				
Ps 77:6	commune							
Ps 78:8		*		*			set aright	
Ps 78:18				tempted				
Ps 78:37				upright iniquity				
Ps 78:72								
Ps 81:12	imagine, lust							
Ps 84:2					crieth			
Ps 84:5				ways of Lord				
Ps 86:11					fear			
Ps 86:12			praise with heart					
Ps 90:12	apply wisdom							
Ps 94:15				upright				
Ps 95:8					harden not			

	Thought	Motive	Spiritual	Moral	Emotion	Physical	Combination	General
Ps 95:10				error in heart				
Ps 97:11				upright				
Ps 101:2				perfect				
Ps 101:4				froward				
Ps 101:5				pride				
Ps 102:4						smitten, diseased		
Ps 104:15					glad			
Ps 104:15b						bread strengthens		
Ps 105:3					rejoice			
Ps 105:25					hate			
Ps 107:12				humble				
Ps 108:1		fixed						
Ps 109:16					broken			
Ps 109:22					wounded			
Ps 111:1			praise with heart					
Ps 112:7			heart trusts					
Ps 112:8	*	*	heart established		*			
Ps 119:2	*	*	*	*	*		whole heart seeks Him	
Ps 119:7	*	*	*	uprightness	*			
Ps 119:10	*	*	*	*	*		whole heart sought God	
Ps 119:11	hid							
Ps 119:32	enlarge							
Ps 119:34	*	*	*	*	*		whole heart keep law	
Ps 119:36	*	*	*	incline, bend				
Ps 119:58	*	*	*	*	*		whole heart pray	
Ps 119:69	*	*	*	*	*		whole heart keep precepts	

	Thought	Motive	Spiritual	Moral	Emotion	Physical	Combination	General
Ps 119:70				fat heart				
Ps 119:80				sound heart				
Ps 119:111					rejoicing			
Ps 119:112				inclined to do				
Ps 119:145	*	*	*	*	*		whole heart cried	
Ps 119:161					stands in awe			
Ps 125:4				upright				
Ps 131:1				haughty				
Ps 138:1	*	*	*	*	*		whole heart praise	
Ps 139:23			God knows					
Ps 140:2	imagine							
Ps 141:4	*	*		*			evil/incline	
Ps 143:4					desolate, astounded			
Ps 147:3	*		*	*	*		God heals broken heart	
Pr 2:2	understanding							
Pr 2:10	wisdom							
Pr 3:1		keep Father's words						
Pr 3:3	write truth in heart							
Pr 3:5		trust						
Pr 4:4	retain words							
Pr 4:21	keep words							
Pr 4:23				keep heart diligently				
Pr 5:12				despise				
Pr 6:14				froward				
Pr 6:18				devise wickedness				

	Thought	Motive	Spiritual	Moral	Emotion	Physical	Combination	General
Pr 6:21	bind							
Pr 6:25				lust				
Pr 7:3	write words on heart							
Pr 7:10					subtil			
Pr 7:25	understanding			wrong ways				
Pr 8:5	wise							
Pr 10:8				wicked				
Pr 10:20				froward				
Pr 11:20								
Pr 11:29	wise							
Pr 12:8				perverse				
Pr 12:20				deceit				
Pr 12:23	fools							
Pr 12:25					heaviness			
Pr 13:12					no hope			
Pr 14:10	knoweth							
Pr 14:13					laughter			
Pr 14:14	*		*	*			backslider ways	
Pr 14:30						healthy		
Pr 14:33	wisdom							
Pr 15:7	foolish							
Pr 15:13a					merry			
Pr 15:13b					merry			
Pr 15:14	understanding							
Pr 15:15					merry			
Pr 15:28	*			*	rejoice		righteous studieth	
Pr 15:30								
Pr 16:1	plans of mind							
Pr 16:5				proud				

156

	Thought	Motive	Spiritual	Moral	Emotion	Physical	Combination	General
Pr 16:9	devise							
Pr 16:21	wise							
Pr 16:23	wise							
Pr 17:16	fool							
Pr 17:20				froward				
Pr 17:22					merry			
Pr 18:2	understanding							
Pr 18:12				haughty				
Pr 18:15			*	prudent				
Pr 19:3					*		Lord vexed	
Pr 19:21	decree							
Pr 20:5	counsel							
Pr 20:9				clean				
Pr 21:1			heart in Lord's hand					
Pr 21:2			Lord weighs heart					
Pr 21:4				proud				
Pr 21:27				wicked				
Pr 22:11				pureness				
Pr 22:15	foolishness							
Pr 22:17	knowledge							
Pr 23:7a	thinketh							
Pr 23:7b	saith							
Pr 23:12	apply							
Pr 23:15a	wise							
Pr 23:15b					rejoice			
Pr 23:17				envy				
Pr 23:19	guide, hear							
Pr 23:26		to give						
Pr 23:33	*			*			perverse, utter	

	Thought	Motive	Spiritual	Moral	Emotion	Physical	Combination	General
Pr 24:2	studieth							
Pr 24:12	pondereth							
Pr 24:17					not glad			
Pr 25:3	unsearchable							
Pr 25:20					heavy			
Pr 26:23			abominations	wicked				
Pr 26:25				rejoiceth				
Pr 27:9					glad			
Pr 27:11								
Pr 27:19				man to man				
Pr 28:14				he hardens				
Pr 28:25				proud				
Pr 28:26	not trust heart							
Pr 31:6					heavy			
Pr 31:11	trusts in her							
Ec 1:13	*	*						
Ec 1:16a	wisdom							
Ec 1:16b	communed							
Ec 1:17	know						seek wisdom	
Ec 2:1	said							
Ec 2:3a		sought						
Ec 2:3b	wisdom							
Ec 2:10a					joy			
Ec 2:10b					rejoiceth			
Ec 2:15a	said							
Ec 2:15b	said	*						
Ec 2:20					*		cause despair	
Ec 2:22	vexed from thinking	*			*			
Ec 2 23		*					not take rest	

158

	Thought	Motive	Spiritual	Moral	Emotion	Physical	Combination	General
Ec 3:11			God set world in heart					
Ec 3:18	said							
Ec 5:2	utter							
Ec 5:20								inner being
Ec 7:2					joy			
Ec 7:3					sadness			
Ec 7:4a	wise							
Ec 7:4b	fool							
Ec 7:7	understanding							
Ec 7:22	knoweth							
Ec 7:25	to know							
Ec 7:26				snares				
Ec 8:5	discern							
Ec 8:9							set to do evil	inner being
Ec 8:11	know	*						
Ec 8:16	considered			*				
Ec 9:1								
Ec 9:3a				full of evil				
Ec 9:3b				madness				
Ec 9:7					merry			
Ec 9:10a	wise							
Ec 9:10b	fool				cheer			
Ec 11:9a								
Ec 11:9b				ways of heart				
Ec 11:10					sorrow			
So 3:11					gladness			
So 4:9a					ravished			
So 4:9b		*			ravished			
So 5:2	*	*					waketh	

159

	Thought	Motive	Spiritual	Moral	Emotion	Physical	Combination	General
So 8:6		set						
Isa 1:5				stoutness	fear			
Isa 6:10a	understand							
Isa 6:10b								
Isa 7:2a								inner being
Isa 7:2b					fearful			inner being
Isa 7:4				pride				
Isa 9:9								
Isa 10:7a	think							
Isa 10:7b	think							
Isa 10:12				stout for bad				
Isa 13:7					melt, fear			
Isa 14:3	said							
Isa 15:5				cry out				
Isa 19:1				melt, fear				
Isa 21:4				fearfulness				
Isa 24:7					merry			
Isa 29:13	*	*	*	*			removed from God	
Isa 30:29					gladness			
Isa 32:4	understand							
Isa 32:6				iniquity				
Isa 33:18	meditate							
Isa 35:4								
Isa 38:3				perfect	fearful			
Isa 42:25	knew not							
Isa 44:18	write							
Isa 44:19	consider							
Isa 44:20				deceived				
Isa 46:8	mind							
Isa 46:12				stout heart				

	Thought	Motive	Spiritual	Moral	Emotion	Physical	Combination	General
Isa 47:7	remember							
Isa 47:8	sayest							
Isa 47:10	said							
Isa 49:21	say							
Isa 51:7				law in heart				
Isa 57:1	not laid to heart							
Isa 57:11	not laid to heart							
Isa 57:15				contrite				
Isa 57:17				forward way				
Isa 59:13	uttering							
Isa 60:5					fear			
Isa 61:1				broken				
Isa 63:4				vengeance				
Isa 63:17			*	*			Lord hardened	
Isa 65:14a					joy			
Isa 65:14b	mind							
Isa 65:17					sorrow			
Isa 66:14	*		*	*	rejoice		whole heart	
Jer 3:10			God's heart		*			
Jer 3:15		*						
Jer 3:16	mind							
Jer 3:17	*			*	*		evil imagination	
Jer 4:4				circumcise				
Jer 4:9a				perish	astonished			
Jer 4:9b								
Jer 4:14				wickedness				
Jer 4:18				wickedness				
Jer 4:19a					pained			
Jer 4:19b					anguished			
Jer 5:23				rebellious				

Verse	Thought	Motive	Spiritual	Moral	Emotion	Physical	Combination	General
Jer 5:24	say				*			
Jer 7:24	*			*			evil imagination	
Jer 7:31	came into							
Jer 8:18				*	faint		deceives	
Jer 9:8	*							
Jer 9:14	imagination							
Jer 9:26				uncircumcised				
Jer 11:8	*		Lord tries	*			evil imagination	
Jer 11:20			Lord tried					
Jer 12:3	*			*			lays to heart	
Jer 12:11		*						
Jer 13:10	imagination							
Jer 13:22	say							
Jer 14:14				deceit				
Jer 15:16					rejoicing			
Jer 16:12	*			*			evil imagination	
Jer 17:1	tablet of heart							
Jer 17:5			departs from Lord					
Jer 17:9				deceitful				
Jer 17:10			Lord searches					
Jer 18:12	*			*			evil imagination	
Jer 19:5	mind							
Jer 20:9	word							
Jer 20:12								God sees heart
Jer 22:17				covetousness				
Jer 23:9					broken			
Jer 23:16	speak							
Jer 23:17	imaginations							
Jer 23:20	thoughts							
Jer 23:26a	heart lies							

	Thought	Motive	Spiritual	Moral	Emotion	Physical	Combination	General
Jer 23:26b				heart deceives				
Jer 24:7a	know	*					return to God	
Jer 24:7b	*	*	*				whole heart	
Jer 29:13			*	*	*			
Jer 30:21		heart to approach						
Jer 30:24	intents							
Jer 31:21		set						
Jer 31:33			law in heart					
Jer 32:35	mind							
Jer 32:39				God give one heart				
Jer 32:40				fear God				
Jer 32:41			God's heart					
Jer 42:20				dissembled				
Jer 44:21	mind							
Jer 48:29				pride				
Jer 48:31					mourn			
Jer 48:36a			Lord's heart					
Jer 48:36b			Lord's heart					
Jer 48:41					pangs			
Jer 49:16				pride				
Jer 49:22a					fearless			
Jer 49:22b					pangs			
Jer 49:23					fainthearted			
Jer 49:46					not faint			
Jer 51:50	mind							
La 1:20					overturn			
La 1:22					fearful			
La 2:18			cried to Lord					
La 2:19			before Lord					

	Thought	Motive	Spiritual	Moral	Emotion	Physical	Combination	General
La 3:21	mind							
La 3:41			unto God					
La 3:51					affected			
La 3:65					sorrow			
La 5:15					no joy			
La 5:17						faint, ill		
Ez 2:4				stiff heart				
Ez 3:7				stout heart				
Ez 3:10	hear							
Ez 6:9				whorish				
Ez 11:19a			God gives one heart					
Ez 11:19b				stony heart				
Ez 11:19c				heart of flesh				
Ez 11:21a				walks wrong				
Ez 11:21b				detestable				
Ez 13:2			prophesy from heart; sinful heart					
Ez 13:17				righteous				
Ez 13:22				*				
Ez 14:3		*		*			set up idols	
Ez 14:4		*					set up idols	
Ez 14:5				estranged				
Ez 14:7		*		*			set up idols	
Ez 16:30			*	languish				
Ez 18:31		*		*			new heart	
Ez 20:16				*			went after idols	
Ez 21:7					melt, fear			
Ez 21:15					faint, fear			
Ez 22:14				endure				

164

	Thought	Motive	Spiritual	Moral	Emotion	Physical	Combination	General
Ez 25:6					rejoiced			
Ez 25:15					despiteful			
Ez 27:31					bitterness			
Ez 28:2a		not set		proud				
Ez 28:2b								
Ez 28:2c			heart of God					
Ez 28:5		set		proud				
Ez 28:6a			heart of God					
Ez 28:6b				proud				
Ez 28:17				proud				
Ez 31:10				proud	vex			
Ez 32:9		*		*				
Ez 33:31							goes after covetousness	
Ez 36:5					joy			
Ez 36:26a			new heart	stony heart				
Ez 36:26b				heart of flesh				
Ez 36:26c								
Ez 38:10	mind							
Ez 40:4		set						
Ez 44:7				uncircumcised				
Ez 44:9				uncircumcised				
Da 1:8		purposed						
Da 2:30	thoughts							
Da 4:16a								not man's heart
Da 4:16b								beast's heart
Da 5:20				proud				
Da 5:21		make like						
Da 5:22				humbled				
Da 6:14		set						

	Thought	Motive	Spiritual	Moral	Emotion	Physical	Combination	General
Da 7:4	guard in heart		*			*	man's heart	
Da 7:28		magnify						
Da 8:25	*	*						
Da 10:12							set, understand	
Da 11:12				proud				
Da 11:27		do mischief						
Da 11:28				against covenant			set, iniquity	
Ho 4:8				*				
Ho 4:11				whoredom				
Ho 7:2	consider							
Ho 7:6		made ready						
Ho 7:11	silly							
Ho 7:14	call out							
Ho 10:2				divided				
Ho 11:8					turned, repent			
Ho 13:6							heart exalted	
Ho 13:8		*		*				God destroy heart
Joel 2:12			turn to Lord					
Joel 2:13			rend your heart					
Ob 1:3a								
Ob 1:3b				pride				
Na 2:10	saith				melt, fearful			
Zep 1:12	say							
Zep 2:15	said							
Zep 3:14					glad			
Zec 7:10	*			*			imagine evil	
Zec 7:12	adamant			*				
Zec 8:17	*						imagine evil	
Zec 10:7a					rejoice			
Zec 10:7b					rejoice			

166

	Thought	Motive	Spiritual	Moral	Emotion	Physical	Combination	General
Zec 12:5	say							
Mal 2:2a	*	*		*			not lay to heart	
Mal 2:2b		*	*				not lay to heart	
Mal 4:6a				turn to children				
Mal 4:6b				turn to fathers				
Mt 5:8				pure				
Mt 5:28	*			adultery	*			
Mt 6:21		*					heart where treasure is	
Mt 9:4	*			*			think evil	
Mt 11:29				meek				
Mt 12:34				evil heart speaks evil				
Mt 12:35				good heart speaks good				
Mt 12:40								heart of the earth
Mt 13:15a	understand			waxed gross				
Mt 13:15b	thought							
Mt 13:19								
Mt 15:8			far from God					
Mt 15:18	mouth							
Mt 15:19				evil				
Mt 18:5				forgive				
Mt 19:8			*	hardness				
Mt 22:37				*			love God	
Mt 24:48	say							
Mk 2:6	reasoning							
Mk 2:8	reason							
Mk 3:5				hardness				
Mk 4:15	word							

	Thought	Motive	Spiritual	Moral	Emotion	Physical	Combination	General
Mk 6:52				hardened				
Mk 7:6			far from God					
Mk 7:19	not understanding							
Mk 7:21	*			*			evil thought	
Mk 8:17	understand							
Mk 10:5				hardness				
Mk 11:23			doubt					
Mk 12:30			love God					
Mk 12:33			love God					
Mk 16:14				hardness				
Lk 1:7				turn				
Lk 1:51	imagination							
Lk 1:66	saying							
Lk 2:19	ponder							
Lk 2:35	thoughts							
Lk 2:51	thought							
Lk 3:15	mused							
Lk 4:18					broken			
Lk 5:22	reason							
Lk 6:45a				good				
Lk 6:45b				evil				
Lk 6:45c	word			good, evil				
Lk 8:12				good				
Lk 8:15								
Lk 9:47	thought							
Lk 10:27			love God					
Lk 12:34	*	*			*		heart where treasure is	
Lk 12:45	say							

	Thought	Motive	Spiritual	Moral	Emotion	Physical	Combination	General
Lk 16:15			God knows heart					
Lk 21:14		settle						
Lk 21:26						failing		
Lk 21:34				overcharged				
Lk 24:25			slow to believe					
Lk 24:32					burn			
Lk 24:38	thoughts							
Jn 12:40a	understand							
Jn 12:40b				hardened				
Jn 13:2		heart to betray						
Jn 14:1					troubled			
Jn 14:27					troubled			
Jn 16:6					sorrow			
Jn 16:22					rejoice			
Ac 1:24	knows							
Ac 2:26	*				rejoice			
Ac 2:37					*		mind, emotion	
Ac 2:46					gladness			
Ac 4:32			believed					
Ac 5:3			Satan filled					
Ac 5:4	conceive							
Ac 5:33	*				*			
Ac 7:23	thought						mind, emotion	
Ac 7:39	change mind							
Ac 7:51				uncircumcised				
Ac 7:54					cut to heart			
Ac 8:21			right					
Ac 8:22	thought							
Ac 8:37			believe					
Ac 11:33		purpose						

169

	Thought	Motive	Spiritual	Moral	Emotion	Physical	Combination	General
Ac 13:22			after God					
Ac 14:17					gladness			
Ac 15:8			God knows					
Ac 15:9				purifying				
Ac 16:14			open heart					
Ac 21:13					weep			
Ac 28:27a	understanding			waxed gross				
Ac 28:27b								
Ro 1:21				darkened				
Ro 1:24				lusts				
Ro 2:5	*			callous				
Ro 2:15				*			law in heart	
Ro 2:29				circumcision				
Ro 5:5			love God					
Ro 6:17	obeyed doctrine							
Ro 8:27		searcheth						
Ro 9:2			to God		sorrow			
Ro 10:1								
Ro 10:6	say							
Ro 10:8	thought							
Ro 10:9			believe					
Ro 10:10			believe					
Ro 16:18	understanding			deceive				
1 Cor 2:9	known							
1 Cor 3:2								
1 Cor 4:5	counsels							
1 Cor 7:37a		stand steadfast						
1 Cor 7:37b		decreed						
1 Cor 14:25	secrets							
2 Cor 1:22			earnest of spirit					

	Thought	Motive	Spiritual	Moral	Emotion	Physical	Combination	General
2 Cor 2:4					anguish			
2 Cor 3:3	tablet							
2 Cor 3:15	vail							
2 Cor 4:6			God shined					
2 Cor 5:12	thought							
2 Cor 6:11	*	*			*		heart enlarged	
2 Cor 7:3	*			*	*		in our heart	
2 Cor 8:16			God put diligence					
2 Cor 9:7		purposed						
Ga 4:6			Spirit in heart					
Eph 3:17			Christ dwell					
Eph 4:18	understanding							
Eph 4:32					tender heart			
Eph 5:19			melody to Lord					
Eph 6:5				singleness				
Eph 6:6			will of God					
Eph 6:22	exhort							
Php 1:7	think							
Php 4:7			peace of God					
Col 2:2					encouraged			
Col 3:15			peace of God					
Col 3:16			Christ dwell					
Col 3:22			fearing God					
Col 3:23			unto Lord					
Col 4:8	exhort							
1 Th 2:4	*	*	God trieth		*			
1 Th 2:17							with you in heart	
1 Th 3:13			God stablish					
2 Th 2:17			Lord directs					
2 Th 3:5			Lord directs					

	Thought	Motive	Spiritual	Moral	Emotion	Physical	Combination	General
1 Ti 1:15				pure				
2 Ti 2:22				pure				
Heb 3:8				harden				
Heb 3:10				err in heart				
Heb 3:12			*	*			not evil heart	
Heb 3:15				harden not				
Heb 4:12	thought							
Heb 4:17				harden not				
Heb 8:10	write							
Heb 10:16				laws in heart				
Heb 10:22a				true heart				
Heb 10:22b				not evil				
Heb 13:9		established						
Jas 1:26				deceiveth				
Jas 3:14				envying				
Jas 4:8				purify				
Jas 5:8	confirm to mind							
Jas 5:15				fatten				
1 Pe 1:22				pure				
1 Pe 3:4								
1 Pe 3:15			God in heart					heart in man
2 Pe 1:19	understanding							
2 Pe 2:14				covetous				
1 Jo 3:19	assure							
1 Jo 3:20a	thought							
1 Jo 3:20b	thought							
1 Jo 3:20c								
Rev 2:23		searcheth						
Rev 17:17			God's will					
Rev 18:7	saith							

172

Appendix B
ANNOTATED BIBLIOGRAPHY

BRAIN

Asimov, Isaac, *The Human Brain.* Boston: Houghton Mifflin, 1963. A popularized treatment of the state of knowledge about the brain. Asimov's evolutionary assumptions and hopes (man would become more than man) need not deter the non-evolutionist from gaining a basic understanding of the brain through this well-written book.

Luria, A. R., *The Working Brain.* New York: Basic Books, 1973. Primary source, covering a lifetime of investigations by this great Soviet neuropsychologist. Broadens the "localization theory" of brain functions and presents some special views held by Luria himself. He recognized that motives, emotions and personality were not yet explained by neuropsychology, but he hoped these areas could be studied too, as that infant science matured.

Sagan, Carl, *The Dragons of Eden: Speculations on the Evolution of Intelligence.* New York: Ballantine, 1972. A popular twentieth century science writer presented a triune model of brain function: 1) midbrain or R-complex, controlling the animal-like abilities, 2) limbic system, controlling emotions, and 3) neocortex, controlling reason. Uses evolutionary explanations. A Pulitzer prize winner.

173

COMPUTERS AND HUMANS

Hofstadter, Douglas R., *Godel, Escher, Bach: an Eternal Golden Braid.* New York: Basic Books, 1979. A highly acclaimed book of thinking about thinking. Says that man's consciousness of self can be explained by physical law. The human mind is a complex computer and computers may yet have human-like "thought."

Weizenbaum, Joseph, *Computer Power and Human Reason.* San Francisco: W. H. Freeman, 1976. A professor who made a name for himself in the computer world argued for the humanity of humans. Computers can never equal them. "It behooves us," he said, "to remain aware of the poverty of our explanations and of their strictly limited scope. It is wrong to assert that any scientific account of the 'whole man' is possible. There are some things beyond the power of science to fully comprehend." A good antidote to the Hofstadter book.

CREATIVITY

Gordon, William J. J., *Synectics: The Development of Creative Capacity.* New York: MacMillan, 1961. The system of bringing together people from diverse fields of specialty to work on solving problems or developing new products. An analogy from one field brings new insight to a problem in another field.

May, Rollo, *The Courage to Create.* New York: Norton, 1973. Presents May's theory of creativity as encounter between the subjective within the person and objective "reality." The merging of the two, which transcends both, is the creative experience. Well written. Readable for everyone.

Rookmaaker, H. R., *The Creative Gift: Essays on Art and the Christian Life*. Westchester, Illinois: Cornerstone Books, 1981. A Christian view of creativity. Inspiration of the Spirit is a part of any creativity which makes a contribution to humanity. Without inspiration, creativity becomes a continual search to find something new. We should use our God-given freedom and not be slaves to legalism.

Rosner, Stanley and Lawrence Abt, Editors, *The Creative Experience*. New York: Dell, 1970. Interviews with highly creative people in both the arts and the sciences. Fascinating insights into how these people work and think.

Ryken, Leland, Editor, *The Christian Imagination: Essays on Literature and the Arts*. Grand Rapids: Baker Book House, 1981. A compilation of essays by many creative Christians. Ryken said that imagination is one way we know truth. For truth—including religious truth—is not solely the province of reason or intellect.

Silvano, Arieti, *Creativity, the Magic Synthesis*. New York: Basic Books, 1976. Surveys major theories of creativity, explains components such as imagery and cognition, examines certain types of creativity, and considers uses of creativity in individuals and society.

HEAD AND HEART

Bettelheim, Bruno, *A Home for the Heart*. New York: Alfred Knopf, 1974. A great psychiatrist described his work in a home for schizophrenic and autistic children. He said, "the more one comes to 'know' intellectually about the patient in abstract form, the less one is in 'touch' with him as a human being." Bettelheim, a survivor of Dachau and Buchenwald, had wonderful insight into the human heart and commonsense ways to deal with children. This is one of several good books by him. Many of his views are close to what we need as biblical views.

Delitzsch, Franz, *A System of Biblical Psychology.* Grand Rapids: Baker Book House, 1966 and 1977. The work of a renowned theologian of the nineteenth century. It has been in English translation since 1899 and is still available to us through the farsighted reprint program of Baker Book House. Our generation may feel it knows more about psychology than Delitzsch's, but this work with its biblical method of learning the psychology of man can still contribute to our thinking.

Lynch, James J., *The Broken Heart: The Medical Consequences of Loneliness.* New York: Basic Books, 1977. "Apparently a peculiar type of intellectual schizophrenia exists between common sense and scientific attitudes when the human heart is considered. Does common sense recognize something that scientists and physicians cannot see?" This book tries to close the schizophrenic gap and show the relationship of such things as love and will to live with the heart.

Poole, Roger, *Towards Deep Subjectivity.* London: Allen Lane, 1972. An exciting book arguing that "objective" science is poverty-stricken. The thought cannot be separated from the thinker. A disappointing ending, that subjectivity should be studied objectively. Man is the measure of things, after all, for the philosopher who believes there is no God.

MEMORY

Adams, Jack A., *Learning and Memory: an Introduction.* Homewood, Illinois: Dorsey Press, 1976. Textbook treatment of important topics in memory. Claims to limit itself to one kind of understanding—the scientific kind. Psychology is defined here, as it so often is, as the science of *behavior.*

Alan, Richardson, *Mental Imagery.* New York: Springer Publishing Co., 1969. A gathering of researches and hypotheses of imagery as it relates not only to memory, but also to thinking more generally.

Baddeley, Alan D., *The Psychology of Memory.* New York: Basic Books, 1976. A good systhesis of earlier memory researches, with the author's interpretations, which help give meaning for the reader. Points out the differences historically between the Ebbinghaus experimental "trivializing" tradition, and the Bartlett wholistic, "experimentally intractable" tradition.

Eysenck, Michael W., *Human Memory: Theory, Research and Individual Differences.* New York: Pergamon, 1977. A compendium of research on memory organized around topics of characteristics of short-term and long-term memory; imagery; retrieval; effects of personality characteristics, anxiety, neuroticism, and aging.

Piaget, Jean and Barbel Inhelder, *Memory and Intelligence.* New York: Basic Books, 1973. A primary source of reports on memory investigations of these great scientists. Supports the Bartlett tradition, that memory depends on internal mental schemata rather than mere associations.

MISCELLANY ON THINKING AND LEARNING

Bettelheim, Bruno, *Surviving and Other Essays*. New York: Alfred Knopf, 1979. Collected essays on many topics by a leading child psychiatrist. How the human spirit handles trauma, such as at Nazi concentration camps, of which Bettelheim was a survivor. An essay on "Education and the Reality Principle," noting the importance of discipline. An essay on art education, also commenting on discipline. Good art is the subjection of creative ability to great aesthetic discipline, not the "undisciplined outpourings of the unconscious."

Glasser, William, *Reality Therapy* and *Schools Without Failure*. New York: Harper and Row, 1965 and 1969. This pair of books presents Glasser's theory, which might also be called "responsibility" learning. The first is written about "mental" patients and delinquents, the second about school children. With the patients, Glasser first diagnosed whether there was a medical problem. If there was not there was no illness, only a need to learn responsibility.

Glasser, William, *Stations of the Mind: New Directions for Reality Therapy*. Cambridge: Harper and Row, 1981. Based on William Powers' Control System Psychology. Ten "stations," or orders of perception, by which we process input from the external world. May help teachers and counselors understand more about how others are seeing their worlds. The tenth station is only a guess that there is a transcendent state of meditation which is outside all the orders of perceiving. Uses the evolutionary terms, "old brain" and "new brain."

Luria, A. R., *Cognitive Development: Its Cultural and Social Foundations*. Cambridge: Harvard University Press,

1976. Observations in the early 1930s in remote areas of central Asia, as village or nomadic peoples were brought into collective farms and socialized labor. Provides a unique look into a kind of thinking not the norm or ideal in our Western society. Primary source material.

Morris, Henry M., *Education for the Real World*. San Diego: Creation-Life Publishers, 1977. The real world is not this present dying world; Christians look for the new heavens and new earth. The Word of God is all from the present world that will survive in the real world. Morris drew his doctrines of education, then, from the Bible.

Wilson, John A. R.; Mildred C. Robeck; and William B. Michael, *Psychological Foundations of Learning and Teaching*. New York: McGraw-Hill, 1969. Textbook style presentation of the Wilson-Robeck three-level model of learning. Integrates numerous existing theories into this model.

INDEX

abstract reasoning, 13, 48, 81,
  89-90, 92, 97-98, 116
Adler, Alfred, 75
Archimedes, 71
Aristotle, 29
Army Intelligence, 126
Art of Thought, The, 74
Asimov, Isaac, 13-14, 173
Bartlett, F.C., 113
*Behavior: The Control of
  Perception*, 14
behaviorial objectives, 44
behaviorism, 9, 17, 21-25, 57,
  60, 95, 120
Bettelheim, Bruno, 47, 49, 66,
  175-176, 178
Beyond Freedom and Dignity,
  22
Biblical learning model, 48
Bloom, Benjamin, 88
brain, 11-13
  pleasure center, 24
  punishment center, 24
Byrd, Randolph, 126
Carnegie, Dale, 114
Cashin, Bonnie, 85
chaos, 76
Chomsky, Noam, 72, 79, 85, 96
Clark, Kenneth, 5, 135
cognitive theory, 25
compensatory theory, 75
concept learning, 48, 53-54, 61,
  66, 86, 90-92, 94, 97, 100-
  105, 131-132
conscience, 34-35, 49, 52, 66
content learning, 46, 87-88, 90-
  91, 97, 109
control theory, 14-15, 59

Courage to Create, 76
Creative Experience, The, 72
Daniel, 29, 79-80
decoding, 94
deductive, 94
Delitzsch, Franz, 2, 29-33, 41,
  176
determination, 17, 52
developmentalists, 26
descipline, 47-51, 62, 78, 127-
  129
discovery learning, 53, 72, 79,
  81, 94
divergent thinking, 74
double seriation, 115
Ebbinghaus, Hermann, 113
ecstacy, 78
emotional life, 36-38
Erikson, Erik, 26
Esther, story of, 98-105
extrovert, 58-59
Eysenck, Michael, 119, 177
falconry, 23-25
Fransen, Ulrich, 84
Galileo, 57
Gestalt theories, 26
Glass, H. Bentley, 83, 84
Glasser, William, 14-16, 59,
  127-128, 178
growth model of learning, 70
Guilford, J.P., 74
Havighurst, Robert, 26
Heart's Code, The,, 124
heart-set, 48, 50-52, 54
Hippocrates, 29
homeschooling, 96, 127, 133
Hook, Sidney, 82, 84
Housman, Alfred, 71